JER

Witches, Ghosts & Traditions

Sonia Hillsdon

SEAFLOWER BOOKS

This edition, revised, reset and redesigned,
published by Seaflower Books in 2002
Reprinted in 2005
Originally published by
Jarrold Colour Publications in 1984

Seaflower Books
16A New St John's Road
St Helier
Jersey
JE2 3LD

www.ex-librisbooks.co.uk

Printed in Britain by
Cromwell Press
Trowbridge
Wiltshire

ISBN 1 903341 13 2

T0 M.K.D. in loving gratitude

Acknowledgements

Miss D. Vincent and Miss C. Jurd, Public
Reference Library, St Helier; Library staff and
History Section members, La Société Jersiaise;
Priaulx Library, Guernsey; Carole and Gary
Owens; Jack du Feu; Howard Butlin-Baker;
Monty Doong; All those who shared their ghost
and other stories.

CONTENTS

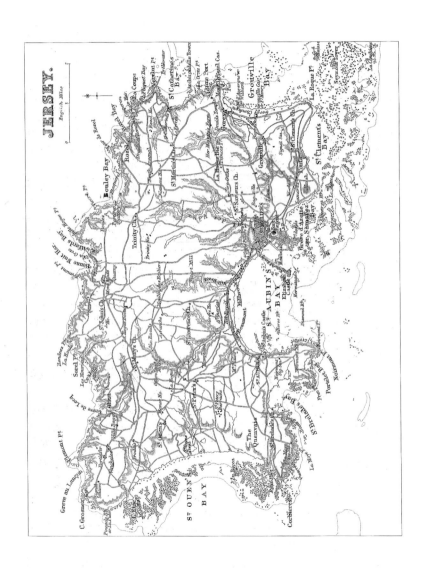

Where it all happened

'Q ueen of the Channel', 'Honeymoon Island', 'The English Riviera'; these are only some of the exotic phrases that have been used to describe Jersey. Holiday brochures boast of its fifty miles of magnificent and varied coastline, the vivid colouring of its granite cliffs, its caves and coves, its twenty miles of sandy beaches – even the charm of its narrow winding lanes.

Its unique flavour derives from both England and France, lying as it does a hundred miles south of Portland Bill and fifteen miles from Carteret. In fact, in its long history it has been ruled by both countries, first France and then England and only after 1900 was French replaced by English as the official language.

Part of Jersey's attraction is its size – nowhere is more than two and a half miles from the sea. And its shape has been described as a 'rectangular biscuit with a large bite [St Aubin's Bay] out of its lower long side and a nibble [St Brelade's Bay] a bit further along.' Yet such is the popularity of this small dot in Mont Saint Michel's Bay that there are now well over 1,000 permanent residents to the square mile. This makes a total population of 87,000, about half of whom live in the capital, St Helier.

Natives and visitors alike have always found flattering things to say about Jersey. As early as 1694 the Island's historian Philip Falle gloatingly noted that Jersey sloped from the north to south, thus trapping more of the sun than northerly-sloping Guernsey. Victor Hugo during his three years' exile here thought the Island 'ravissant'. George Eliot on holiday here in 1857 wrote of 'Such grassy vallies in this delicious island, with sleek cows turning mild faces on us as we pass them: such shadowy lanes and glimpses of the sea at unexpected openings!'

Despite some adverse changes since then – tower blocks and the coming of the car – Jersey seems to have lost none of its allure as a holiday resort. Every year thousands of tourists visit the Island, the grassy isle or *Gers ey*, as it is possible our Scandinavian ancestors called it.

There is, however, another side to this 'land of sunshine, sparkling seas and hot white sand'. The sun does not always shine; in a storm the seas smash against the shores; and there are just as many miles of repelling cliffs as there are of inviting sand. The flow of the sea round the Island is frequently checked by the weird shapes of low-lying reef and giant boulders jutting up many feet above its surface. The landscape is often dominated by the indifference of bleak sand-dunes or stark promontories.

Even in 1798 an intrepid Englishman who sailed here from the Isle of Wight noticed these more Gothic aspects of Jersey. St Brelade's Bay was 'bound by barren rocks where even moss declined to grow, whose native cliffs worn away by Time and the beating Surge, wore Horror's Forms; the land retreated from the sea with sterile aspect, a few scattered trees bowing their blasted heads.' As he travelled north up the coast to St Ouen, he noted in his diary 'all was a desert before us, now and then a clump of rushes marked the poverty of the soil'.

Horrifically shaped rocks, wracked trees, trackless desert – if these were the impressions of St Brelade and St Ouen on an urbane traveller from the eighteenth century, what effect would these menacing features, together with other wild parts of Jersey, have on a sparse population of ignorant, illiterate Islanders in the Dark and Middle Ages?

On the south they had at that time marshy land crossed by numerous streams, making it impossible to get even the short distance from St Helier to St Aubin, except across the sands at low tide. To the north from Gronez to Rozel there are the sheer forbidding cliffs, which at their highest point reach 500 feet. To the west are the bleak dunes of St Ouen, to the east yet more forbidding promontories. To increase the inaccessibility of many parts of the Island in those carless, roadless days the whole interior is crossed by mainly north-to-south-running deeply indented valleys.

And all around – the merciless sea, a sea whose power to shape and reshape the Island gave rise to many strange tales. For in Neanderthal times this oblong rock we call Jersey was once part of Europe and was either surrounded or completely covered by the great Forest of Scissy. Then over the following thousands of years the sea, as it fell and rose during the various Ice Ages and their aftermaths, began its insidious encroachment. First came the division of Jersey from England and finally the severance of Jersey's link with the mainland of France.

So our ancestors had, as we have today, the sunken remains of those prehistoric times to marvel and wonder at. For when there is a very low tide at St Ouen's Bay and other conditions are favourable, weird shapes of black tree-stumps can be seen. This so-called 'submerged forest' is all that is left of that once great stretch of prehistoric oak trees.

From the dawn of modern history, therefore, Jerseymen have always been isolated by the natural features of their environment. They have been separated from one another, even until Victorian times, by seemingly large tracts of alien and hostile terrain. They have been denied easy and frequent access both to Britain and France by their own treacherous coastline and the surrounding sea, and there is nothing like isolation for encouraging belief in the supernatural!

Pouquelayes or Fairystones

Another factor fostering the credulous beliefs of Jerseymen, besides their isolation from each other and the rest of the world, has always been the mysterious remains of prehistory. Although the Islanders of Jersey were, at first, baptised Catholics and, later on, strict followers of Calvin, they had on every side pagan relics as huge focal points for their imagination.

Massive, mostly unhewn, blocks of stone marked sites which could once have been pagan temples. Some of these sacred places were also used, either by the same group of early man or his later descendants, as burial-places for those most venerated by the tribe. However, their attraction as ritual centres did not stop in prehistoric times. Quite a few of these upright stones (menhirs) and the burial chambers (dolmens) have continued to have a role to play in the supernatural belief of the Islanders until comparatively recently.

In some instances, the inexplicable presence of these pagan stones, as they stood massively upright in many different parts of the island, often far from any quarry from which they might have been hewn, was explained by fairy magic. As it appeared to the descendants of prehistoric man that they could not have been shifted to their present site by any human agency, it seemed obvious that they had been borne through the air by fairies – carried in their magic aprons!

The north coast gives an instance of this association of magic with prehistory. Between Les Platons – at over 400 feet above sea-level the highest point in the island – and Vicard Point overlooking Bouley Bay, there are at least three sites with prehistoric links. At Les Platons there is a large mound under which were discovered two urns holding the charred bones of a child and a woman. Below Belle Hougue is a cave in which animal remains from prehistoric times were found while on a rocky ledge at Vicard Point is what appears to be a menhir lying on its side – La Pierre de La Fételle.

It is no coincidence that in this same area there are also links with fairies and magic properties. The fallen stone, now La Pierre de La Fételle, used to be called La Roche à la Fee – both meaning the fairy stone, while the name of the field in which it lies is Le Clos de la Pouquelaye – the fairy stone enclosure. Then the spring which is found on the promontory of Belle Hougue – La Fontaine ès Mittes – has a charming part-pagan, part-Christian legend attached to its supposedly magic properties.

The word *mittes* is Jersey Norman-French for naiads, those watery sprites whose special task it was to guard springs and fountains. Two of them, apparently, came to Jersey and their names were Arna and Aiuna. They lived most happily for several centuries on the promontory of Belle Hougue, tending its spring. Their home was a rustic grotto on whose mossy floor they had their simple meals; their view was the gorse- and heather-covered cliffs with the frothing sea below.

Yet it had been agreed from the beginning of their Jersey sojourn that these two naiads would not be allowed to live on earth forever. So one autumn day, as they were sitting on the cliff-top watching the dying rays of the setting sun, an angel came to them in a brilliant white light. With burning eyes he told them that their days at Bell Hougue were over and that they had been summoned by God to spend the rest of time near his throne beyond the stars.

Arna and Aiuna rose willingly from their grassy seat to do the angel's bidding. But as they began their ascent to heaven, they remembered the many happy hours they had spent on this beautiful spot and from each of the naiads fell a tear of regret.

These two tears dropped into the spring that flows to the sea from Belle Hougue and from their purity came twin blessings that would forever be associated with the spring. Water from La Fontaine è Mittes, so legend tells us, has the magic properties of both bringing back sight to the blind and the power of speech to the dumb.

There are two other prehistoric sites with similar fairy associations. To the east of the island, in the Parish of St Martin, there is Neolithic passage grave with a massive capstone weighing nearly twenty-four tons. It is known both as the Dolmen de Faldouet and La Pouquelaye de Faldouet. Just south of this dolmen is the road name Rue de la Pouclée.

The second pagan relic to be taken for a fairy stone is the menhir which stands in a farm on the northern outskirts of St Helier. It is the origin of the name of the road La Pouquelaye and also the nearby Pouquelaye Gardens.

In the time of the Lieutenant-Bailiff Jean Poingdestre there were still at least fifty such Pouquelayes and not just singly but in clusters. It is interesting to read how he describes these 'Monuments of Antiquity' in his *Discourse of the Island of Jersey*, written in 1682:

> The most ancient are those wee call Poquelayes, which consist for the most part of foure huge stones, whereof three planted on end Triangle-wise at foure, five or six foot distance from each other, and the fourth flatter then ye rest and soe large as being layd on ye top of them three to beare on them all, and to make a vault under: then at ten or twelve foot distance, sometimes more sometimes lesse, another great stone set up in ye manner of a pillar. Of these Poquelayes some are yet entire, others are fallen and peeces of them sunck into ye ground.

He then goes on to describe two Pouquelayes which he considers different from the other groups of fairy stones:

> I observe two different in forme from the rest; one in a place called Les Landes Palot, not farre from the Free Schoole, consisting of one onely massive entire stone, and therefore not

hollowe under as ye rest, which seems to be ye naturall rock growne upon the place, and by art hewed and fashioned into a naturall Poquelaye; but yet it is separated from ye rock under it with such a counterpoise, *that at a certaine place a boy with his finger's end can move it*; which a hundred men could not otherwise doe. The other is to be seene neere ye old Castle as you goe towards St. Catherines. This stands just at the Top of a round hillock made of hands and is supported, not by three, as the rest, but by five stones, which by length of time are suncke soe deepe into the ground, that a man must creepe to goe under it; ye covering being exceeding large and weighty.

His speculations as to the use of these Pouquelayes and the pagan rites he imagines were associated with them are even more revealing:

I take them to have been sett up for Altars upon hills and open places and many times neere the Sea, to offer Sacrifices Sub Dio to the Earth or some Planet. I say by those Poquelayes seeme to be signifyed some Rites of that time not common to the Continent, where noe such stones are to be seene, that I can heare of. And that those stones served for Altars I am ye apter to beleeve because that at ten or twelve foot distance from them there is still another stone not soe high as the rest, planted up in the manner of a Desk, where I conceive the Priest stood performing the usuall ceremonies while the sacrifice was consuming; and secondly because that under those Stones or thereabouts have ben found in ye earth certaine round Rowes of Stones, with perfect ashes in the middest of them; and sometimes a litle stone fashioned into the forme of a Smiths Anvill, noe bigger then a mans fist. All which things seeme to shewe that those monuments served for the Idolatry of those times.

It is interesting to note that when the word 'Dame' appears in Jersey place-names, it has different meanings according to which word precedes it. If 'La' precedes Dame, as in Rue à la Dame (the road near the Rocking Stone), then the lady referred to is a fairy. If 'Notre' precedes Dame, then the reference is to the Virgin Mary, as in the chapel – Notre Dame des Pas.

The Legend of Hougue Bie

As well as many of the stones and burial chambers of prehistoric man becoming part of Jersey folklore, so did some of the surviving mounds which covered the Neolithic and Bronze Age dead. They were called 'Hougues' from the Norse word *Haugr*, meaning a mound. The most famous of the Hougues in Jersey is La Hougue Bie in the Parish of Grouville and linked to it are both pagan and Christian associations. This huge forty-foot-high mound with a diameter of 180 feet is probably not only the most impressive relics of early man in Jersey but also one of the most remarkable dolmens in western Europe. Yet, unusually, this extensive cruciform burial-chamber is the site of only one tomb.

Some thousands of years later, two Christian chapels were built on the top of this pagan mound. The reason why the first chapel was built is told in a romantic legend that probably explains the name of the Hougue as well.

In the Dark Ages, when there was a great marsh in the Parish of St Lawrence, a dragon lived there wallowing in the mud and breathing out destructive bursts of fire. The news of the devastation it was causing in Jersey – where no one seemed to be able to check its ravages – eventually reached Normandy and the ears of the Seigneur of Hambye, a Norman knight.

Nothing daunted, and having taken a loving farewell of his wife, Hambye set sail from Normandy with his faithful squire, Francis, to see if he could deliver Jersey from its terrible scourge.

After a great fight and with one final thrust from his mighty sword, the knight did just that. With another slash he cut off the dragon's head to prove his victory. Then, tired from his exertions on behalf of the Islanders, he decided to lie down for a rest before setting sail for Normandy and his beloved wife.

Then came the moment of betrayal. His seemingly loyal squire suddenly plunged his dagger into his sleeping lord's breast. For it was his plan to claim the dragon-slaying as his own and, with this valiant deed to his credit, win the hand of the beautiful Lady Hambye whose love he had always coveted.

Leaving the body of his master hidden in Jersey, the perfidious squire set sail – with the dragon's head – for Normandy. There with downcast eyes he told Lady Hambye that the dragon had, alas, killed her husband and that he, Francis, had himself slain the beast in revenge for his dear lord. Then, to bring further persuasion to his tale, he added that just before he died Seigneur Hambye, greatly impressed by his squire's brave deed in slaying the dragon, gave him as the most fitting reward his own wife's hand in marriage.

The widow believed every word of this wicked tale. With her blood still cold from the horror of what she had heard and her voice failing on her lips, she nevertheless consented to become the bride of Francis in deference to her husband's dying wish.

Now comes the final twist to the tale. One night, it is said, the new husband gave away his true character as a murderer by talking in his sleep. Immediately the betrayed wife had him hanged for his heinous crime and once the concealed body of her first husband was found in what was then the Parish of St Saviour, she caused it to be covered by a mound so high that she could see it from where she lived in Normandy.

On top of the mound she had a chapel built, dedicated to Notre Dame de la Clarté – Our Lady of the Dawn. Here Masses were to be said for her murdered husband's soul. It is said that she died still gazing out across the sea at her husband's memorial mound;

and so from this lady's faithfulness to the memory of her first husband could have come the name by which we know the mound today, La Hougue Bie – from La Hougue Hambye.

In 1509 a second chapel was built beside the first, which later writers claimed was full of fraudulent tricks to get money from the superstitious poor. When the Island was still Catholic, the then Dean of Jersey, Richard Mabon, had the Hambye Chapel restored as a thanksgiving for his safe return from a pilgrimage to Jerusalem. With the sights he had seen in the Holy Land still clear in his mind, he then had a second smaller chapel built alongside, which became known as 'Jerusalem.' Below he had a crypt made as nearly resembling the Holy Sepulchre as he could remember it.

Many pilgrims then began to visit Hougue Bie to worship in Richard Mabon's two chapels and to visit his crypt. Later, Protestant detractors suggested that he made quite a thriving business from them. For example, there was a statue of Our Lady placed in an alcove whose hand was outstretched to receive alms. When the coins fell through a hole in her hand, they touched a spring which made her hand move as though in gratitude for the gift.

Another trick to bring in the offerings, according to one writer, was to proclaim a miracle. 'He hid in the wick of candles a very thin wire, which he fastened to the roof of the Chapel. The smoke from the flame made the wire invisible, and the candles seemed to float in mid-air, and people believed that they were held by the virtues of Our Lady.'

Not all the rites and rituals associated with prehistoric remains were, though, as innocuous as fairy magic or a belief in miracles. In common with Britain and the rest of Europe, some of these menhirs and other naturally impressive rocks attracted devil worship and witchcraft. One such notorious centre for black magic was the forty foot-high granite rock on Le Nez point in St Clement called 'Rocqueberg'. That it had been struck by lightning and had what looked like the prints of a cloven hoof on one of its ledges all pointed to it being the haunt of the Devil. But more about this Witches' Rock in a later chapter.

The Islanders Themselves

*A*ccording to the historian Balleine, your true Jerseyman is 'intensely un-English, yet even more intensely anti-French'. Yet he may speak to his family in a version of French which the Duke of Normandy, William the Conqueror himself, would have understood. He also has customs – such as the Clameur de Haro – which would have been part of William's Norman heritage, too.

So what exactly is the origin of your true Jerseyman? Opinion is still hotly divided and there is at present a wordy battle going on between those who claim the Normans as their true ancestors and those who believe that the Bretons are. Most historians, though, would agree that after the disappearance of the cavemen from their settlements at La Cotte à la Chèvre and La Cotte de St Brelade, there were two main waves of immigration until 933, when Jersey became part of the Duchy of Normandy.

The first to arrive on Jersey's shores about 7,000 BC was a race of pre-Celtic origin, often misnamed as Iberian. They were small, swarthy and, predominantly, tillers of the soil. Though they themselves lived in mud huts, they buried their dead in enormous stone tombs, many of which – as we have seen in the last chapter – remain marvels of construction to the present day.

Next to land were the tall, fair-haired Gauls, who, with their superior iron swords and javelins, had conquered their way from the Danube, across France to Normandy and finally made the Iberians in Jersey their slaves. They were famed for their religious fanaticism in following the bloodthirsty rites of the Druids. At their open-air altars they appeased the gods of earth and sky with human sacrifices, often burnt shriekingly alive in huge basket cages.

Then came the most important invaders to stamp their characteristics on the genetic heritage of the Jerseyman – the pirating Vikings. For almost the whole of the ninth century the Islanders had cause to dread the summer months. For then it was that the Scandinavian looters came in their long boats to ravage the coasts of both France and England – taking in the Channel Isles en route. Not only did the savage raiders set fire to the houses of Jersey and murder its inhabitants, they even broke into their sacred places – the prehistoric tombs – for buried treasure. The few small wooden Christian churches that had been established by various missionaries were also razed to the ground.

It was not only in Jersey, though, that the Viking pirates struck terror. Charles the Simple of France had watched these men from the North – or Normans as they were called – impudently sail up the River Seine to besiege Paris itself. Against such superior force the siege was only lifted by a hefty ransom. Therefore, when the French King wanted to secure peace for his subjects who were being terrorised in the Rouen area by the pirate chief Rollo, he knew that bargaining was the only method open to him.

So it was that a treaty was signed in 911 between Charles and Rollo which was to affect the whole history of Jersey to the present day. For, by the Treaty of Clair-sur-Epte, Rollo was bought off to keep the peace with that part of France round Rouen we now know as Normandy – the Norman's land. In his son's time the Channel Islands were added to the Duchy, and that is how, from 933 to 1204, Jersey came under Norman rule.

> *I craîe en bas coume la coue d'une vaque.*
> *He grows downwards like a cow's tail.*
> (Facetious reference to a person of stunted growth.)

The Norman Inheritance

Once the former raiders of Jersey became its possessors, they turned from their barbaric and lawless ways to become devout Christians and fanatically law-conscious landowners. In fact, this litigious trait of Jerseymen – even today – is summed up in the saying, 'They will go to law almost for a potato!' The way in which the Normans also dropped their Scandinavian language in favour of French, the original language of Normandy, can be seen by the difference between some coastal and inland place names.

As Viking raiders they gave Norse names to coastal land marks – for example L'Etac and L'Etaqueral from *stakh*, meaning a high rock. To the interior, which they divided into feudal fiefs and ruled as Seigneurs, they gave mainly French place-names, such as La Garenne – a rabbit warren, or Maufant – bad mud.

Two interesting anachronisms can be traced directly back to this Norman rule of Jersey. The Islanders owe allegiance to the Queen of England through the English sovereign's ancient title of 'Duke of Normandy'. So their loyal toast is, 'The Queen, Our Duke!' A Jersey/Norman French version of the National Anthem begins:

Dgieu sauve not'Duchêsse
Longue vie à not'Duchêsse
Dgieu sauve la Reine!

Yet King John, way back in the thirteenth century, was the last King of England to have the right to call himself 'Duke of Normandy'!

The second Norman custom is to raise 'La Clameur de Haro' when a Jerseyman wants to stop somebody from doing harm to his property (or, formerly, to himself) until an independent court can judge between them. The procedure is for the aggrieved person to fall down on his knees, bareheaded and in the presence of two witnesses, also bareheaded, to cry out, 'Haro! Haro! Haro! à l'aide, mon Prince, on me fait tort,' (Haro! Haro! Haro! to my aid, my Prince, I am being done wrong!) On hearing the cry, the aggressor must stop at once from what he is doing until the case has been decided in a court of law.

The word 'Haro' is believed by some to be a direct appeal to Rollo or Rou, the first Duke of Normandy – 'Ha! Rou!' Others think that 'Haro' is just an exclamation like 'Help!'. The cry itself is not used all that frequently and, even then, sometimes wrongly. In August 1972 Mrs E. Bailhache was fined £50 for raising the Clameur de Haro incorrectly; in April 1977 Mr A. Robertson was removed from the Royal Court after only getting as far as kneeling and crying out 'Haro! Haro! Haro!', because his case was going to be heard anyway.

A successful Clameur in the 1970s was that raised by Mrs A. Touzel on 4 May 1974. She called the Prince to her aid, down on her knees in front of two witnesses in a field in St Ouen. It was to stop a man lifting potatoes he had wrongly planted in her mother's côtil (field). When the case was heard in the Royal Court, the man was fined only £1 with £5 costs because there had been a genuine mix-up over boundaries. Nevertheless Mr Vernon Tomes, Solicitor-General at the time, said that he was satisfied that the Clameur was properly raised as it concerned possession of property and was the very type of case for which the Clameur was designed.

Three men who have clearly seen Norman traces in the Jerseyman's make-up are Victor Hugo, the Reverend G. R. Balleine and Dr Frank Le Maistre. In his novel *Toilers of the Sea*, Victor Hugo commented on their similar appearance: 'There is something especially attractive in the Jersey and Guernsey race. The women, particularly the young, are remarkable for a pure and exquisite beauty. Their complexion is a combination of the Saxon fairness, with the proverbial ruddiness of the Norman people – rosy cheeks and blue eyes.'

In his *Bailiwick of Jersey* (1970), Balleine notes the similarity of characteristics. 'The typical Jerseyman today, in his sturdy independence, his self-reliance, his shrewdness at a bargain, his tremendous industry, his reticence, his thrift, is almost the exact counterpart of the Norman across the water.' There is a warning, though, from the compiler of the great *Dictionnaire Jersiais-Français*, Dr Le Maistre, that all those who claim to be direct descendants of these Norman colonisers of Jersey may not in fact be so. To be a 'vrai Jersiais' in his opinion you must bear a name and speak the language known to your forebears and have at least 600 years of their undiluted blood in your veins!

Other Immigrant Ingredients

The qualifications to be called a true Jerseyman according to Dr Le Maistre are of such a tall order that many Islanders must look to more recent immigrations. From the sixteenth to the nineteenth centuries France was again to be their source. During the time of the Religious Wars in France, from 1562 to 1598, numbers of French Protestants, or Huguenots as they were called, fled to Jersey to escape persecution at the hands of the Catholic rulers of France. So to such Norman names as De Carteret, Le Maistre, Vibert were added the Huguenot ones of Girard, Gosset, De la Place and Hemery.

At the end of the eighteenth century came the refugees from the French Revolution, but, more importantly, from the 1850s onwards came the Bretons. It is to this Celtic race that many Islanders look for their ancestors. Their forebears could date as far back as Christian Britons, fleeing religious persecution by the Anglo-Saxons in the sixth century, who eventually settled in what became known as Brittany. Some of them certainly settled here en route for the French mainland. Or their family trees could be traced to the nineteenth century immigrations of agricultural workers, for many stayed on after 14 July each year, when harvesting here was over and the French Government expected them back to gather in the harvests in Brittany.

These Breton workers have been described as impervious to fatigue, quite happy with belly pork, strong onions and cider for nourishment, and straw in the barn for a bed. For the sake of the extra money, they were even willing to work from three in the morning until nine at night! The historian Saunders sees more of a similarity with the Bretons than with the Normans: 'The Islanders like the Bretons are small, dark, tenacious of old customs and less inclined to ostentation than their neighbours in Normandy.' They have left names such as Genee and Le Breton.

Seasonal farm workers from Brittany have, since the 1970s, been replaced by an annual Portuguese contingent. At the end of the season their lovingly cared for cars are a familiar sight as they start the long journey home. Their possessions, most newly acquired, are piled high inside and tied precariously to the roof rack.

Some people believe that the last and most pervasive of all immigrations – from the U.K. – is only a post-Second World War phenomenon. In fact, fleeing to Jersey as a tax haven began as early as the 1820s, when no income tax and a regular steamship service made the Island that much more attractive and accessible. Even by 1840 the English residents numbered as many as 15,000. So spread the new immigrants' language and currency: pounds, shillings and pence took the place of *livres tournois* in 1834, while English ousted French as the official language in 1900. French is, however, still used in the Courts for such procedures as prayers and oath-taking.

Edward Gastineau in his *Hobble Through the Channel Islands* in 1858 crisply describes the mongrel breed resulting from these several immigrations. According to him they are 'deficient both in stature and beauty'! Furthermore, he points out, 'the greatest characteristic of the people of this island is frugality carried to its extreme limit, and designated by many writers as penuriousness; … that money, or rather the getting of money, is the principal thought that occupies, from blushing morn to dewy eve, the whole mind of the population.'!

Il a un yi au ciel, l'autre sus ses échus..
He turns one eye heavenwards, the other on his money-bags.

Les Crapauds and Les Anes

Whatever a Jerseyman's good or bad qualities, he will tell you that he is worth ten of any Guernsey 'ane'. A Guernseyman, on the other hand, has equal contempt for the Jersey 'crapaud'!

'Ane', 'crapaud', - how did the natural rivalry between the two islands come to be expressed through such nicknames? A

Jerseyman will tell you that 'donkey' needs no further explanation – all Guernseymen are stubborn. Why Jerseymen should be called 'toads' is a longer story.

One legend has it that in time past, when meeting saints was an everyday event, two of them happened to bump into each other in Guernsey. There, by a stream in the Parish of Castel, St George met St Patrick. Ireland's patron saint had just come over from Jersey where he had been pelted with stones and told in no uncertain terms that he was not wanted. He had already found a far warmer welcome in Guernsey and was thinking of calling the island his own when he had met St George. He, too, had been thinking along the same lines because of the kind reception he had received.

Rather than have an unsaintly argument as to who actually had first claim to Guernsey, the two saints decided that neither of them would keep the island. But they agreed that each should give, before they left, some lasting benefit to the hospitable islanders.

St George immediately looked down at the stream by which they stood and blessed it. Its waters were forever to have the power of healing. More than that, whomsoever owned the land through which the stream ran, so long as he kept the water from being defiled in any way, would never go hungry, nor would his children. The stream was thereafter known as St George's Well and was believed by all Guernseymen to be superior in its efficacy to any other healing waters on the island. In fact, so well worn did the path to it become, that in 1408 an Act was passed prohibiting its use except for those who had to go that way to church or who genuinely wished to be healed.

St Patrick, not to be outdone and thinking to give their just deserts to both islands at the same time, filled his wallet with all the nastiest Guernsey creatures – such as snakes and toads – that he could find. He then went back to Jersey and emptied them all out so that Guernsey would be free of everything noxious but Jersey would have a double share – especially of toads!

Another version is that St Sampson, Guernsey's Patron Saint, banished moles, serpents and toads from his island so that the

Sarnians would better despise the Jerriais. No matter, the result was and remains the same.

That St Patrick, or St Sampson, did his work well is testified to by the seventeenth-century Poingdestre: 'This Island is noe lesse annoyed by several sorts of vermine, creeping and crawling things, than damnifyed by the wind and ye water. It is scarce credible what quantity we have of Toades, snakes, slowe wormes, rats and mice, with their Enemyes the States.'

But trust a Jerseyman to turn even the large and ugly 'Crapaud Bufo' to his advantage. Only a few years later the historian Falle was to agree that 'the only blemish and disgrace of the Island (as 'tis by some accounted) is the great multitude of Toads which swarm in it and are chiefly seen in Summer and moist Weather', but he goes on to explain, 'The notion our people have of them, is, that they draw out what is noxious and impure in the Elements, and thereby contribute to health; and this they pretend to prove by the contrary example of Guernezey, which will not suffer a Toad to live in it, and yet is thought not so healthy as JERSEY'.

Even though the Island's 'blemish and disgrace' had given the Jerseyman his nickname of 'Le Crapaud' – toad, it was still put to profitable use. When a monthly magazine was first published in April 1835 it proudly bore the title *The Crapaud* and had a toad on its front cover.

Today, however, a Jerseyman thinks of himself less as a toad than a bean. It is thought that this nickname came about because of the much-loved bean crock being the Island's special dish. A boost was given to the name in the early 1970s when a soft toy was produced called the 'Jersey bean'.

The traditional rivalry between Jersey and Guernsey has not just been a matter of exchanging nicknames. Even their coats of arms are different – albeit by mistake! The copier of Edward III's seal of legality for use by the Channel Islanders gave an accidental extra flourish when he came to Guernsey's seal. So Jersey's three leopards appear on a plain shield, while Guernsey's three prance on a sprigged one.

Then on two important occasions they have taken opposite sides. In the sixteenth century Guernsey accused Jersey of

No. 1,   Vol. I.

THE CRAPAUD.

Toad that under the cold stone,
Days and nights hast thirty-one,
Swelter'd venom sleeping got.

SHAKESPEARE.

APRIL, 1835.

JERSEY :

PRINTED AND SOLD FOR THE PROPRIETORS, BY P. PAYN,
ROYAL SALOON,

employing ministers of religion that their Governor had expelled. The resulting acrimony resulted in religious and diplomatic relations being broken off for eight years!

Castle Cornet

During the Civil War in the seventeenth century, Guernsey had mainly Parliamentary sympathies, while Jersey remained loyal to King Charles. When the few Guernsey Royalists barricaded themselves in Castle Cornet for eight years, it was, naturally, Cavaliers from Jersey who smuggled in food and provisions for them. So it is no coincidence that it was a Guernseyman, Dr Hoskins, who, in the nineteenth century, spread nasty rumours about this island's Margaret de Carteret and her supposed affair with the Prince of Wales, later Charles II, during his ten-week exile in Jersey.

Today the rivalry has tamed down to such taunts as a Guernseyman's short legs and the Guernsey proverb: 'Qui epouse Jerriais ou Jerriaise, Jamais vivra a son aise', which roughly translated warns, 'If you want a quiet life, never take a Jersey wife! or husband!' It is only at the traditional Muratti matches that it flickers into vivid life again – thanks to Mr Edward Lander.

In 1905, when Mr Lander was agent for the then world-famous Muratti cigarettes, he suggested an annual football contest between Jersey and Guernsey, sportingly adding Alderney to make it a three-cornered contest. A silver vase, the prize to be played for, was specially made in London at a cost of £20. Before a gate of 2,000, in the April of that same year, it was won by Guernsey, who beat Jersey in that first Muratti match, 1-0. Needless to say, as the referee happened to come from Guernsey, he had to be afforded police protection as he left the Jersey ground! Not surprisingly it was also the last time that a Channel Islander was asked to referee a Muratti match.

One of the most amusing tales to spring from 'les crapauds' versus 'les anes' shows just to what lengths a Jerseyman will go to try to prove his superiority. There were once, apparently, three stalwart sailors who came to Guernsey from Jersey with a boatload of farm produce to sell. They did extremely well and decided to spend their profit on a jar, or two, of Guernsey cider. It then came to them as they drank what a good idea it would be to carry off Guernsey and join it on to St Ouen. No one would ever miss such a tiny island from the English Channel and it would look well in St Ouen's Bay when it arrived there at first light.

So the Captain of the Jersey boat, Maître Ph'lip, ordered his cousin Pierre to make the hawser fast to one of the sharp tips of rock on St Martin's Point. This done, the sails were hoisted and the three men burst out singing

> '*Hale, Pierre! Hale, Jean*
> *Guernsi 'sénvient.*'

as the boat gave Guernsey its first tug to float it off over the short distance to St Ouen. But much to the sailors' astonishment, the hawser suddenly snapped in two, throwing them all to the bottom of the boat. Much bruised and shaken by this unexpected turn of events, they had a serious discussion as to what to do next. They then solemnly decided not to renew their attempts and simply to leave Guernsey where it was!

Some Jersey Customs
Then and Now

Family Occasions

Special occasions need special customs and they were seized upon by the hard-working Islanders as a break from everyday routine. Just as their frequent intermarriage has meant that 'J'nos accouosinous, car touos les jerriais sont couosins' (We call each other cousin, for all Jersey people are cousins), the great family occasions played, and still do play, an important part in their lives.

First then the customs associated with birth, marriage and death. The birth of a baby was marked by a gift in a popular metal silver. The godparents in particular would buy, often from the local silversmith, one silver spoon for a boy, or six if it were a girl. A more lavish present would be a Christening bowl or cup.

These silver Christening cups are unique to Jersey. The bowl of four inches in diameter and one and a quarter inches deep has a decorated handle either side but, unlike its Guernsey counterpart, has no foot. The initials – usually scratch-engraved – would sometimes be syllabic initials, such as MGF for Mary Godfray, instead of the simple MG. Silver porringers in the British style, or handleless beakers – introduced into the Island by the refugee Huguenot silversmiths – were sometimes used as Christening gifts, too. Today the traditional Jersey bowl is still a popular choice for both Christenings and Marriages.

There used also to be a less expensive but more symbolic gift given to the new-born baby. If an egg was placed in its hand as its very first gift, the baby would forever be guarded against poverty. If the egg was kept, it would always be a talisman of good luck.

Mrs Carré still has the brown egg given to her by her father when she was born Iris Florence Pinel on 18 February 1929. Her father wrote both her name and the date on the egg and it has been one of her treasured possessions ever since. Wrapped in a silk handkerchief, then placed carefully in a cardboard Easter Egg, it has accompanied Mrs Carré on all her travels, even as far as Australia.

Jersey names for boys have included Amice, Pierre, Helier – even Winter, as shown by the former Constable of St Peter, Winter P. Le Marquand. For girls there have been Collette, Rozelle or the more common Jeanne. It was eventually considered unlucky to continue the custom of giving a new baby the same name as a brother or sister who had died in infancy. The friends and relatives of the family would drink to the baby's future in 'L'ieau d'cannelle' – cinnamon water strongly fortified with white brandy!

More silver teaspoons marked an engagement. The young man would not only present his fiancée with the ring but also a gift of some value. This was often in the form of a dozen or half dozen teaspoons, perhaps even a pair of silver sugar-tongs – all with his fiancée's maiden initials engraved upon them.

But the best excuse for great feasting and merry-making was the marriage itself. After the service there was a huge midday meal, traditionally consisting of roast beef, ham, plum-pudding and the cake – 'gâche à corinthe'. The hordes of relatives and friends packed into the home of the bride's parents would, having drunk cider with their meal, toast the happy pair – usually in mulled wine.

Then everyone would dance far into the night, only stopping for a breather when neighbours fired their guns outside the house in a 'feu de joie' and had to be rewarded with liquid refreshment. The first Sunday after their wedding, the self-conscious newly-weds were expected to go to church to 'pay their regards'.

Firing guns obviously used to be the done thing on wedding-days. When in 1663 Philippe Payn rode from Grouville to St Lawrence to claim his bride Susan Hamptonne, not only was he accompanied by a great number of guests from the Island's noblest families but he was saluted by cannon- and musket-fire all along the route. At the bride's house more gun-fire, followed by a half-hour's speech by the Dean of Jersey before they all set off for the ceremony at St Lawrence's Church. Then the St Lawrence parish cannon was let off. During the homeward journey back to Grouville, through every parish the newly-weds went, more cannons were fired – even a few salvoes from Elizabeth Castle! Certainly a memorable if rather noisy day for the new Mrs Payn.

Even sixty years ago shotguns were still in evidence at some weddings. Mr Arthur Jandron and his wife Alice had a guard of honour formed by neighbours carrying shotguns, when they got married in St Peter's Church in 1923.

Tangible evidence of some of those long-ago marriages can still be seen in the wedding-stones often found over the front door of old Jersey houses. These show the initials of the bride and groom and a date. The initials of Philippe Payn himself were carved on the stone put by his parents on their house La Maletière at Grouville. This showed not only his parents' initials and the date 1635, but also the family's arms and the initials of Philippe and his brothers.

The date, though, on these wedding-stones is not necessarily the date of the wedding itself. It could record alterations, or an extension, to a house, even some thirty years after the marriage. From about the middle of the eighteenth century, marriage-stones also often included the carved interlocking of two hearts.

stone at La Maletière of JEAN and MARIE PAYN, and their sons JEAN, FRANÇOIS and PHILIPPE.

J. Stevens

A death in the family also had its special customs. In the house the body was on view to any callers, the windows would be shuttered and the mirrors covered. Then friends and relatives would bear the coffin – covered with laurel and ivy as symbols of immortality – to the churchyard. Those living in St John's Parish would have been reminded, as they are to this day, to get ready for the funeral by the five-minute tolling of the bell at eight o'clock on that morning. Parishioners would know that one toll was for a man, two for a woman and three if the deceased were a child. The bell also served, so it is said, to remind St Peter to get the gates of Heaven open in readiness.

After the funeral service and burial would come the 'dîner d'enterrement' – the funeral meal. This was accompanied by plenty to drink, which could somewhat change the initially sombre mood! The Sunday after the funeral, the mourners were allowed to remain seated throughout the service and this custom was known as 'Prendre le deuil' – taking mourning.

But the deceased's power to affect his family and friends does not necessarily end with his death. There is still the Will. And in Jersey, as the laws of inheritance are still to some extent based on 'Le Grand Coustumier du Pays et Duche de Normandie', they are rather unusual. There was nothing untoward about leaving money for a suitable funeral sermon to be preached, nor for the poor to be remembered but other bequests were, to some extent still are, hedged about by legal considerations.

For example, if land or property was to be left it could not be inherited by a non-Britisher. They could only receive money from the sale of the land or property. Nor could a man leave his widow without provision, no matter how bad a wife she had been. She was allowed life enjoyment of a third of all landed property owned by her husband. Any children inherited on the ratio two-thirds to the sons and a third to the daughters, with the eldest taking the home. All wills were open to challenge for a year and a day after being registered.

Today anyone from anywhere in the world can inherit from a Jersey resident. But though a man may now bequeath his real estate to whomsoever he wishes, a third of the rest of his wealth must still go to his wife as her dower right. Another third will go to the children but the rest may go to the inheritors of his choice. Wills are still open to challenge for a year and a day.

But these old laws of inheritance did mean that many an old Jersey granite farm remained, and still remains, in the same family from the day it was built.

Bouon Appétit

There are certain foods which are Jersey specialities. The most sustaining of typical Island dishes is Jersey Bean Crock and there is still a shop-window in St Helier which displays bowls of the different kinds of dried beans necessary for its making. For this 'Piot et des Puis au Fou' you soak a quarter-pound each of haricot, butter and broad beans overnight. After the soaking, the beans are put into an earthenware crock with a pig's trotter or piece of belly pork, covered with water and cooked in a low oven for seven to eight hours.

If you still had room, then your next course could be one of the many dishes made from locally caught fish: casseroled oysters; fried ormers, razor fish, or sand eels; boiled whelks or mussels; limpet omelette; baked conger cutlets; soused mackerel; spider crab or lobster.

In the cake line there are two Island specialities – vraic buns and Jersey wonders. In the days when whole families went to collect seaweed (*vraic*) as a fertiliser or fuel, they would need to work hard and quickly to get it all cut from the rocks before the tide came in. To keep up their strength they had yeast and raisin buns to eat, with cider. Hence the name 'vraic buns' – from the occasion, not the ingredients! When baking these buns, or any bread for that matter, it was customary in some households to make the sign of the Cross on them before they were put in the oven.

Jersey Wonders – a type of superior doughnut in a figure of eight or butterfly shape – are still a great favourite at fêtes and bazaars and are at their best when absolutely fresh. It is said that to assure the success of your Jersey Wonders, it is best to make them when the tide is on the way out!

At recent popular revivals of Le Vier Marchi (the Old Market) set up in the Royal Square, where it always used to be until 1800, Jersey Wonders are often sold by stallholders wearing the traditional Jersey sun-bonnet. This 'câpote' is closely linked to the type of bonnet found in Normandy and was worn when fruit-picking, vraicing and doing other outside jobs.

The framework of the bonnet is looped canes over which the material of the wearer's choice is stretched. The frill from the bottom of the bonnet goes right down to the shoulders, giving ideal protection from the sun, and the four strings are tied in two bows under the chin. Such a resilient bonnet was ideal for milking because, when the milker was resting her head against the cow's side, the canes would fold back but not break, while her hair would still be protected by the *câpote*.

Other High Days and Holidays

Once the palm trees have had their leaves tied back to withstand the worst of the south-westerlies, there are quite a few leisure-time activities to get an Islander through the winter. Not all these pursuits go back to the distant past but they have already become traditional for many Islanders and their children in the 1980s. Visitors to Jersey find these customs of today, because they are in many cases unusual, as interesting to hear about as customs of yesterday. For those who enjoy an exhilarating cross-country ride there is the Drag Hunt which has meetings every Thursday and Saturday from October to March. The unique element about this hunt that so pleases anti-blood-sport supporters is that there is no blood, no fox, no hare – nothing, in fact, but a scent to follow. A cloth is permeated with a made-up scent and then dragged along a cross-country route by a couple of members on foot or on horseback, for the hounds to pick up. The sport was started over a hundred years ago by the British Garrison Battalions and today attracts an average of thirty to forty riders each meeting, with a special hunt for the younger children four or five times a year.

For the artistically, musically, or dramatically inclined, for many years now it has been the custom for children and adults alike to enter the Eisteddfod. Despite its Welsh name, it is the show-case for home-grown talent to display itself before U.K. adjudicators. The climax of the three weeks used to be the Grand Festival Concert held at the Opera House on the last Saturday in November. Here, before a packed house, appear the top of each class in music, speech, mime, dance, French and Jersey Norman French: winners of such honours as the W.A. de la Mare Perpetual Trophy, the Joan Le Sueur Memorial Medal, the Le Poidivin Cup and the Jeannette Boielle Award. Since 1984 the Eisteddfod has been held in the spring, at the same time as the Arts and Crafts section.

Until 1914, November used to be remembered for its Black Butter Nights. 'Du Nier Beurre' is a traditional preserve made in huge quantities. The following ingredients are used in this Grouville Parish recipe:

Tante Elizabeth by Edmund Blampied (La Société Jersiaise)

10 gallons of cider	24 Sliced lemons
20 lb of sugar	700 lb of sweet apples
3 sticks of finely chopped liquorice	3 lb of allspice

During the day the women of the neighbourhood would peel and cut up every one of the hundreds of pounds of apples, while the men and children would gather enough wood to keep the fire going non-stop for nearly two days. Once the fire was lit, usually in the afternoon, a huge pan (eune paile) was put on it to boil the cider until it turned to jelly. Then the cut apples were gradually added, with the men stirring all the time, so the slices would not stick to the bottom of the pan and burn. The other ingredients were added at least two hours after the last batch of apples had been stirred in, except for the spice, which was added in the last ten minutes.

This cooking went on all night and well into the next day, with everyone taking turns to tend the pan and mend the fire. The heat had to be well regulated the whole time, for as one recipe records 'This preserve has extraordinary spitting power and will reach every corner of the kitchen with the slightest encouragement'! When neither stoking nor stirring, everyone would dance and sing and make free with the plentiful refreshments always provided. It was 'a time of jollity and fun only understood by those who were there'.

Once the preserve was cooked, it was stored in crocks for use until the next 'Séthée D'Nièr Beurre' – the following November. Today the Young Farmers' Club and St Martin's Methodist Chapel are two groups which continue this now almost lost tradition of black butter making and they count it as one of the highlights of their social calendar.

Christmas Customs

To the traditional Christmas festivities known in the U.K., Jersey has added a few of its own. For example, for twenty years now it has been the tradition for Father Christmas to fly into the Island. Once here, he visits every Parish in turn to collect as many second-hand toys in good condition from the children of the Parish as he can. Nearer Christmas these are given to other less fortunate children.

A much older custom, now sadly discontinued, is 'La Longue Veille'. Jersey folk, men and women, had always been fanatical knitters from the Middle Ages, so much so that, at its height, important farming activities were being neglected. In 1606, therefore, an ordinance of the Royal Court forbade anyone to knit during vraicing or harvest-time on penalty of a heavy fine.

Nevertheless, by the middle of the seventeenth century, with up to 6,000 pairs of woollen stockings a week being produced in Island homes, those that were exported to England were already known as 'Jersey socks or stockings'. Eventually any knitted fabric came to be known as 'jerseys'. The main difference between a 'jersey' and a 'guernsey' nowadays, by the way, is that the traditional pattern knitted in the sister isle has no anchor incorporated in the front panel under the neck as the Jersey one has.

The long winter evenings, starting with 'L'Assise de Veille' in the first week of September, was the time when most of the knitting was done. Before the days of electric or gas light, the knitters would gather together in each other's kitchens – never the same one two nights running by the hanging light of the oil-wick 'crasset'. Sitting on the 'veille', an early type of sofa filled with dry bracken, or the larger jonquière, they would pass the knitting-time with gossip, telling stories, singing, eating 'lard au fou' (bacon) and drinking cider – all by the blaze of a crackling, dried vraic fire.

The most important 'veille' of them all was 'La Longue Veille' – the long sitting-up – on the 23 December. This was deadline date, as all the knitted garments had to be finished in time for sale at the Christmas Eve market. But no matter how long the knitters stayed up to get everything done, there was still time for merry-making before the long night was through.

The tradition of Les Veilles, which over the centuries gradually diminished to a purely social occasion – without the obligatory knitting-needles – continued right up until the First World War. Today some Parishes still hold 'une veille' during the winter as a fund-raising event, or merely as an excuse for a parochial get together.

Christmas Eve, Christmas Day

Christmas Eve in Jersey shares a charming observance with some parts of the mainland. It is considered extremely unlucky to enter a cowshed or cowstalls on that evening, in case you happen to chance on the cattle kneeling ready for their obeisance to the Infant Jesus as the clock strikes midnight. That this belief was held in Hardy's Wessex, too, is seen from his poem 'The Oxen.'

It was not, though, until the nineteenth century that Jersey quite threw off the Calvinist convention that Christmas was originally a pagan festival and, therefore, not to be enjoyed. But, in the 1800s, it began to adopt the festivities that were gradually being associated with 25 December in England. Already in 1834 it was reported that it was customary for the Islanders to have a whole week of feasting and merry-making at Christmas-time.

In those days of large families, twenty to thirty relatives would get together for a gargantuan meal of fresh pork, roast beef, goose and puddings. Then there would be 'Mountains of cakes to accompany tea'. All this feasting would be followed by exciting games of cards or dominoes – played for sous or, later, halfpennies!

To get everyone into the festive mood, there had long been a tradition in some parishes of ringing the church bells non-stop from midday on Christmas Eve to midnight on Christmas Day. In the Parish of St Mary, though, the bell-ringers unfortunately got out of hand – they overdid the alcoholic refreshment between pulls! Many rectors had objected over the years but had always been overruled. But there was one rector who was quite determined to put a stop to this age-old custom – for one thing he wanted a time of silence in which to conduct a Christmas service.

In 1868, after several unsuccessful attempts, the Reverend Le Couteur Balleine thought at last he had outwitted the over enthusiastic bell-ringers. He crept up to the belfry and first removed the bell-clapper, then the bell-rope and, finally, the ladder to the belfry itself. As a double precaution he even changed the locks on the church doors!

The fury of the bell-ringers when they turned up to find themselves locked out of their own church can well be imagined.

Immediately a handbill was written and circulated, telling the parish that their rights were being taken away – 'Enfants de St. Marye vos droits sont envahis'. Then under the leadership of Sorsoleil, the Church Warden, the bell-ringers took retaliative action. While the church door was being kicked in, one of their number rode post-haste to St Helier to fetch rope and another dashed to a blacksmith for him to hammer out a rough-and-ready bell-clapper.

The result was that not only did the frustrated Rector then have to listen to his church bells, clanging away without a break from ten o'clock on Christmas Eve till four on Christmas morning, but he also found the church in a disgusting state after a mammoth drinking session! Nor, when he complained that once again he was unable to hold a Christmas service, did he get any backing from the Parish Assembly. 'If there were any disturbances', it righteously noted, 'it was entirely due to the pigheaded behaviour of the Rector who wished to deprive the inhabitants of a right which was dear to them'.

Today the custom of bell-ringing at Christmas is continued in the parishes of St Mary, St Ouen and St Peter – but there are now gaps so that church services can be held!

For Jersey children, Christmas Day itself used to be a chance of getting extra pocket-money. It was a popular ritual for them to go round the neighbourhood begging 'Noue! Noue! mon Noue, s'il vouos plait'. – 'Christmas! Christmas! My Christmas box, if you please'. The custom seems now to have completely died out but, as late as 1966, Mr P. Ahier records that the cry was still being heard in St John.

Who would imagine that St Helier's Signal Station on Fort Regent would become a traditional part of the Island's Christmas? Yet every Christmas morning since 1973 from this nearly 300-year old station are hoisted eighteen fluttering flags spelling out in plain language 'Season's Greetings'. Even more impressive is the illuminated cross, some forty foot high and thirty foot wide, that is erected there each Easter and Christmas. Every night of the festive season, this shining symbol can be seen, not only along the coastal plain to St Aubin but right round the east of the Island to Grouville and as far out to sea as Les Minquiers.

When it comes to New Year's Day, as well as it being a propitious time for sowing parsley, and an unlucky day for having a woman as the first visitor, it has a taboo still strongly adhered to by many Jersey families. No one must wash their hair or their clothes on New Year's Day. If they do, they wash a member of the family away. As recently as 1982 when a young girl was found out to have washed her hair on 1 January the others in the family could hardly bring themselves to talk to her for the rest of the day.

Traditional Activities in Spring and Summer

Low water fishing has been a Jersey way of life for centuries, with the fish to be had as small as shrimps or as large as lobsters. When it came to lobster-catching, there was once a fisherman who did particularly well at it. But he kept it a closely guarded secret just whereabouts in the rocks he found the fish, even from his family. One day the fisherman fell ill and, when he realised he was dying, he decided at last he would reveal his secret. So he had himself carried to the rocks and there, for the first time, showed his son the exact crevice where he had caught so many lobsters.

A sight that has many tourists wondering is that of the natives, at some such sandy beach as the St Aubin's Fort area or Le Hocq, with salt in one hand and a plastic bag in the other. They, believe it or not, are hoping to entice razor fish to pop their heads above the sand and be caught. A more unsporting way is to dig them up with an umbrella spoke!

Prawns, winkles, limpets, sand-eels, ormers, crabs, lobsters – all there at low water to be taken by the frugal Jerseyman who does not like to see anything go to waste. Even more fun than going for the ormers when there is an 'r' in the month (and using the shells for decoration afterwards) were the sand-eeling parties, which took place once the potatoes had been planted. In strict Calvinist times this typical Jersey pastime afforded particular delight of a non-fishy kind when the moon was full and there was plenty of liquid refreshment in hand. So much so, that in 1589 the Royal Court had to pass an ordinance stating that in order to safeguard the morals of women and girls, they were forbidden to take part in sand-eeling at night, except when in the company of their husbands or parents. Matters, however, were no better a hundred years later, when Poingdestre noted that sand-eeling 'was wont to be a great pastime for young people who flocked to it, not so much for the fish, as for divertissement and many times for debauchery for which cause these meetings have been discountenanced and are at present less frequented'. The daylight parties, though, were real family affairs. Sidney Bisson records how 'all the relatives, neighbours and friends would drive down to La Rocque in their dogcarts or old box-shaped Jersey vans. The old people brought their knitting and sat on the rocks near the slipway, telling each other stories of the phenomenal catches they had once been young enough to make.'

Dr Le Maistre remembers the sand-eeling parties at night, down on La Grève au Lancon in St Ouen (Plémont Beach). 'They came with forks and rakes and the "hotte" [a special implement peculiar to the St Ouennais] and lanterns, sometimes more than a hundred of the latter all over the beach – truly a fairy-like and enchanting scene from the heights above.'

In the 1870s and 1880s the first Sunday in May meant a special treat for 'les villaises' – the townees. It was the custom for the young people of St Helier to get up at sunrise and walk to the farms on the town's outskirts. There they would drink milk still warm from the cows they had watched the farmer milk. One of the favourite haunts was Vallée des Vaux, where there used to be a house called 'Milk Punch House', because some of the young people would drink milk punch near there. To make this refreshing drink they needed three-quarters of a glass of fresh milk, two teaspoons of sugar, one wine glass of brandy, and one pinch of cinnamon.

Since 1945, the most heartfelt celebration of the whole year – certainly for the older generation – comes on 9 May. It was on this day that, as Winston Churchill himself put it, 'our dear Channel Islands' were liberated from nearly five years of German occupation. On 9 May 1945, the Bailiff, Alexander Coutanche, was rung from Guernsey, which had already been freed, asking him to take Jersey's Military Commandant, General Wolfe, out to the British destroyer *Beagle*. There, on board, the formal surrender of the many thousand German troops occupying Jersey was signed.

On the public holiday of 9 May, there is always a Thanksgiving Service at the Town Church in memory of that day. In the afternoon, the final of the Muratti football match between Guernsey and Jersey is usually held. Those attending either event could very well pass by the letter V, carved in the paving of the Royal Square, that also commemorates those Occupation years. Under the very noses of the Germans, 'Vega 1945' was carved, in recognition of the visits during the spring of 1945 of the Swedish Red Cross ship *Vega*, whose food parcels literally saved the Islanders from starvation.

The next two events are enjoyed by Jersey's summer visitors as well as the residents. In July, against the breath-taking scenery of Bouley Bay, is the famous Hill Climb. Motor-cycles and light cars have been making the mad dash up the winding road to the top since the early 1930s, though the official National Hill Climb has only been run since 1957.

And the biggest crowd-puller of all Jersey's annual events? August's Battle of Flowers – naturally. It started as part of a continental-type carnival to celebrate the Coronation in 1902 of Edward VII and Queen Alexandra. Victoria Avenue was the venue, with a gun positioned on Westmount to signal the beginning and close of the festivities.

As the procession moved down the avenue, there really was a 'battle', though waged with true Edwardian decorum. As the local paper of the time reported: 'Occupants of the carriages were well supplied with ammunition in the form of tiny bunches of flowers and at once opened a fusillade on their friends in the stands. The fire was returned with energy and the battle soon extended nearly the whole length of the Avenue and on both sides.'

But there must have been spoil-sports even in those more elegant times, for only two years later, the Official Programme warned: 'All flowers used must be free from Thorns and Hard Stems and must on no account be wired. Flowers must not be thrown at drivers or horses'! On later occasions the crowds got so out of hand that they tore apart the beautiful floral floats they had come to see.

An early Battle of Flowers, in 1912.

All that unpleasantness – and the break in continuity because of the two world wars – is now over, with many changes effected since then to make the Battle of Flowers a major attraction for summer visitors. The night before, they enjoy going behind the scenes to the large warehouses and garages where hordes of helpers stick the thousands of individual flower heads in place on a wooden or metal framework. On the day itself, they marvel at the finished floral designs, as the floats move in procession along Victoria Avenue. They are led by a Miss Battle of Flowers and her escort from show business, Mr Battle, on their own specially decorated float.

One of the last traditional events in Jersey's yearly calendar, before it is time to tie up the palm trees once again, is Battle of Britain week. This special occasion may be celebrated in many places on the mainland but the air display that is always staged in Jersey on the Thursday afternoon – a half-holiday – can rarely have such an impressive backcloth as Elizabeth Castle. To see first the veteran war planes fly sedately over this Tudor fortification and then the Red Arrows roar in front and then divide either side of it, with their red, white and blue trails of smoke behind them, is a truly memorable sight.

The War with the Devil

The Catholic Way

The battle against the Devil began sometime in the fifth and sixth centuries. It was then that the Celtic Christians were forced to leave the west of England and Wales, to make their escape from Anglo-Saxon persecution and to seek safety in Brittany. On their way there, many visited or stayed permanently in Jersey.

Poingdestre, writing in the seventeenth century, sees those early days, not as a universal conversion of the Island to Christianity but only as a 'good step' towards it.

> As for Christian Religion it is not easy to marcke precisely the time of its first beginning in these Islands: for questionlesse it came not in all at once, by a General Conversion, noe more then in other parts. It was first preached or taught in secret, then more openly, when it had gott the favour of some protection, then it was recommended, but not forced; till at last, Paganisme being decryed and quite subdued, it was established by Lawe. It found a mighty obstacle to its growth in the Irruptions of Goths, Vandalls and other Northerne people, which fell upon those times; soe yt. it could not be perfectly free till ye. Reigne of Clodovoeus, first Christian King of France, who authorised it by his example, yet soe as Paganisme was still permitted and long after practised.

The first Christians from that time who made their mark in Jersey are the quartet of saints – Sampson, Magloire, Marcouf, and Helier. St Sampson is remembered both from a chapel dedicated to him at La Rocque and a revealing anecdote. It is said that the Jersey children he met while here so much preferred to take part in the pagan rights associated with the Winter Solstice on 22 December, that he actually had to bribe them with a medal to entice them away to attend the Feast of Christ's Nativity instead!

As St Sampson is mainly remembered in connection with Guernsey, so is his cousin, or nephew, Magloire mainly associated with Sark, where he set up a monastery with over sixty missionaries. Yet it is thought that he and his monks also established religious communities here – on the north coast at Grève de Lecq and at Bonne Nuit, both natural landing-places from Sark. The founding of the Priory of St Mannelier in St Saviour is also attributed to him, as the Islanders knew the Saint as Mannelier rather than Magloire.

About 525, it was St Marcouf who recommended the Belgian Helibert, later known as Helier, to come to Jersey – not as a missionary but as a hermit. Later, the Celtic Saint came to see how his proteégé was faring in his lonely cave in St Aubin's Bay, near to where Elizabeth Castle is now.

It is said that during Marcouf's visit, Jersey was threatened by a fleet of pirate ships from the Orkneys. To avert the attack, he and Helier knelt down and prayed with such efficacy that the pirates began to fight viciously among themselves, so that in the end not one was left alive.

An alternative version is that, alerted by the raucous sound of Scandinavian war-songs, Marcouf and Helier, surrounded by a group of frightened Islanders, saw about 3,000 invaders sailing towards them. As they landed, there was an ominous clap of thunder, so the Islanders, horrified both by what they saw and heard, began to run for their lives. But suddenly they were transfixed, for there was St Marcouf making the Sign of the Cross and urging them to attack the invaders, not flee from them. The invaders were, apparently, so terrified by the imposing stance of the Saint as he urged his force forward, that they fled back to their ships, many of which were lost in the ensuing storm.

The legend of the Belgian hermit, St Helier, belongs to the section on the Parish to which he has given his name. But these three missionaries were the first in the long line of those who tried to win the Islanders from their pagan ways. They taught them a clear distinction between good and evil, painting sharply contrasted rewards in the Christian concepts of Heaven and Hell. To keep them on the narrow path of righteousness were the angels: to tempt them to the wide ways of wickedness was the Devil.

According to the Christian Church in Rome, one way to avoid the snares of the Evil One was to meet together for the saying of prayers and for taking part in the Christian Sacraments. This was done first in small wooden chapels, forever being burned down by pagan invaders, and then, after the turn of the eleventh century, in larger, stone churches.

Another way was to build a chantry chapel, where a priest could be hired to be in constant prayer for the safe-keeping of the chapel owner's soul and the souls of his family. In Jersey these chapels were simple constructions of rough stones, with narrow lancet-windows and the only ecclesiastical furniture an altar-slab and a basin to wash the vessels used at Mass. They were built by as many as could afford them, because Islanders believed they were one way of ensuring the soul's escape from the torments of Hell, or from a long time languishing in Purgatory.

La Chapelle ès Pecheurs

One of the few chantry chapels still in existence is the one at St Brelade. Known as La Chapelle ès Pecheurs, the Fishermen's Chapel, the family who owned it kept it solely for their own use. Sometime during the fourteenth and fifteenth centuries they decorated its walls with Biblical scenes, such as the Annunciation, the Crucifixion and the Resurrection.

A further method for a well-to-do Catholic to atone for his sins and make good his account with God was to go on a pilgrimage. In Jersey, the rock where St Helier used to live became a Pilgrimage Centre. This custom was revived sixty years ago, taking place each July. A popular shrine abroad for Islanders to visit was that of St James of Compostella in Spain. In 1428 alone, no fewer than sixty licences were issued to Jersey Pilgrims to make this journey, despite the Hundred Years War still being waged.

The badge worn by pilgrims to Compostella was of a scallop shell and two reminders of that famous shrine can still be seen in Jersey. There is a scallop shell on an alcove in St Saviour's Church as testimony that the Parish Constable had been there, and also on the fine silver-gilt dish at St Brelade's Church, brought back by a pilgrim from Compostella. Such an important part did pilgrimages play in the life of the Islanders, that Victor Dupont sold his property just so that he could 'go on the holy voyage' – to Rome.

For poor and rich believers alike, a constant reminder of the power of good over evil was the symbol of the Cross. Not just in churches, in homes, on rosaries, but in little clearings by the side of roads and paths. The many wayside crosses that used to be all over the Island are now remembered only by place-names: Les Hautes Croix, La Route ès Croix, La Croix Varin are just three. At these wayside crosses it was the custom for the men to doff their hats, and all to bow their heads and make the Sign of the Cross, as they still do in some parts of Catholic Europe today.

The fiercest battle against the Devil these saints and their followers had to wage was, as we have seen, against the continued veneration by Islanders of pagan menhirs, dolmens and tumuli. In the same way that this cult lasted in Brittany right into the twentieth century, so in Jersey, until comparatively recent times, was it hard to eradicate.

The whole Hougue Bie legend could, in fact, be read as a victorious phase in this particular battle. The story of the Dragon slain by Seigneur Hambye could just have been a symbolic way of recording that a pagan chief in St Lawrence was finally slain by a

Christian from Normandy. The Chapel of Our Lady of the Dawn built by his widow could have been a seemingly God-given opportunity to change a pagan monument into one of Christian significance.

A logical result of believing in the Devil's opposition to the will of God was to categorise people's actions as belonging either to one or the other; but how to decide the inherent evil or good of what someone had done? In the early Middle Ages, a most horrifying method was devised which was called 'The Judgement of God'.

The theory behind the method was simple – God, or good, will always triumph. So four tests were thought up to prove the theory. If, for example, there was a dispute between two of the landed gentry, then the outcome would be decided by a trial of arms. The two disputants would either meet each other to do battle themselves, or would select champions to fight for them. Whoever won the battle had obviously been in the right all along – for God looks after his own. Such a 'trial by battle' was ordered by the Bailiff to take place on 10 August 1494, between the Seigneur of St Ouen and the Governor of Jersey's henchman, Le Boutillier. The outcome can be read in the section on St Ouen's Parish.

Three other trials which came under 'The Judgement of God' were trials by the Cross, Water and Fire. In the first, the litigants would have to stand in public with their arms outstretched in the form of a cross. Whoever would keep this holy position the longest would be deemed to be in the right, whether it be to a claim of property or to continue living.

The next two trials were similar in their barbarism. In the trial by water, a heavy weight was placed at the bottom of a cauldron which was then filled to the top with water. In front of a dozen witnesses, the water was then brought to boiling-point. Once this was reached, the accused had to plunge his hand into the boiling water, bring out the weight and carry it nine feet. This done his hand was bound and kept bound for three days. If, when the sealed bandage was taken off, there was any sign of scalding then the accused's guilt was assured. For the trial by fire almost the same ritual was laid down:

A red-hot iron will be presented to the accused which he must take in front of everybody and which he must carry for the distance of nine feet. Then his hand will be wrapped up and sealed so that it can only be unwrapped after three nights. If it is healthy then he can render glory to God, if it is festering he will be judged guilty.

As John Ahier comments in his *Tableaux Historiques de la Civilisation à Jersey*, some Islanders 'found certain substances which stopped the burning action, which rubbed on to the hands enabled them to carry hot irons.' Therefore, he continues, 'the innocent were certain to be burned and the rascals had impunity.'

The impact of centuries of Catholicism on the island was frankly analysed by the non-Catholic historian, Falle:

If a people of themselves religiously disposed (which I beg leave to say has been sometime our Character) are not there withal competently knowing and enlightened, they will naturally give into everything that has a shew of piety, be it never so idle and childish. Such was our State under Popery, no place being more overrun with little and low superstitions than this Island.

Leunne se Samedi et fille de prêtre
Ne veinnent qu'eunne fais les sept ans.
Saturday's moon and priest's daughter
Come but once in seven years.

The Calvinist Way

Then came an unexpected twist in this war against the Devil. The tables were suddenly turned and the prosecutors themselves became the prosecuted. Ten centuries after Christianity came to Jersey, it was the turn of the Catholic faith itself to be seen as of the Devil and ousted from the Island.

All over Europe the Gospel teachings of Christ had become increasingly overlaid with superstitious beliefs and dubious ritual. Then, in the sixteenth century, men like Luther in Germany and Calvin in Switzerland began to protest against the materialism and malpractices of the established Church in Rome. They demanded a return to the simple austerity and truth of the Early Church. Their protest and their demands started the Reformation – a religious movement that affected Jersey even more rigorously than it did England.

In France these protesters, or Huguenots as they were called, adopted as their mentor the strictest reformer of them all – Calvin. They believed that, in their endeavours to return to what Christ taught, they were actually involved in a life-and-death struggle with the Devil. The Catholic Church in France simply regarded Calvinists as heretics and had them burnt. Many of those who escaped this persecution fled to Jersey.

Two decades later, England – and, therefore, Jersey – in their turn began to feel the full effect of the Reformation. After the death of Henry VIII in 1547, the posts of Governor of Jersey and Protector of the Kingdom were filled by the Duke of Somerset, uncle to the nine year-old King, Edward VI. Somerset was a militant Reformer and by 1548 the zeal of his anti-Catholicism was already at work in the Island.

His first target was the practice of hiring a priest to say Masses for the dead. So, at one stroke, with the passing of the Chantries Act, all chantry chapels were closed and all payments for Masses to be said and candles to be lit confiscated. Some of these disused chapels can still be seen today as the cottages they became.

Next issued were Royal Injunctions for the immediate destruction of all objects of superstition. The wayside crosses which had been venerated for centuries were hewn down without a qualm. From the parish churches was wrested everything that smacked of Popery. Stained-glass windows, statues, altars, fonts were all smashed – even murals were effaced from the walls. Church bells, chalices, censors – anything that had a marketable value was sold for the King's profit. Cleared of all traces of devilish idolatry, the churches were then whitewashed and transformed into austere Huguenot temples.

So zealously did the Reformers in St Brelade do their destructive work, that they tore out the font and threw it down a nearby hill. There it lay for 300 years, hidden in the bracken, until in 1843 a party of picnickers found it and it was eventually restored to the church.

It is also recorded that, on 22 May 1563, all Catholic religious books had to be brought to St Helier market-place to be burned. The wood needed for this purging bonfire had to be paid for and transported by the books' owners.

Yet was this wholesale destruction of the outward signs of their centuries-old Catholic beliefs accepted without question by the Islanders? The objectors recorded are so few, that the answer must be 'yes'. So for nearly a hundred years, Calvinism was the State religion of Jersey. It had received advance publicity from the refugee Huguenots; exiled French Protestant clergymen were on hand to become its ministers; Calvin's austere Book of Church Order became its law.

The most pervasive element of Calvinism – which

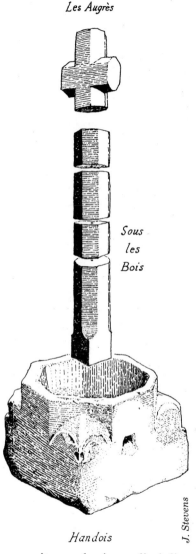

Les Augrès

Sous les Bois

Handois

J. Stevens

some claim persists to this day – was its emphasis on discipline. Calvin himself had said, 'doctrine without discipline is like a body without a backbone', and it was not just the Sabbath that was hedged with restrictions. Elders were appointed to keep an eye on the everyday activities of the families in their care. Did they have family prayers morning and evening; say grace both before and after meals? Did they indulge in any sinful pursuits, such as dancing or the singing of lewd songs? If transgressions such as these were not spotted by the Elder, neighbours were expected to inform on each other and bring such backsliding to the notice of the Parish Consistory, which met every Sunday following Afternoon Service.

The Sabbath was the day when Calvinism made quite sure that Jersey families had hardly a minute to spare from Temple-going in which they might, mistakenly, enjoy themselves. As soon as the Temple bell stopped ringing, every one had to leave whatever they were doing and hurry to take part in the service, in which the only music would be the singing of metrical Psalms. Once at the Temple, the men and women separated, entered by different doors and sat on opposite sides, facing the pulpit. From this dominating position, the Minister preached long sermons to his flock in the morning and catechised them in the afternoon. Wholly forbidden on the Sabbath were hunting, cards and dice, nor could taverns remain open during the hours of Temple-going. There was even a prohibition recorded on the Rolls of the Royal Court in 1602 in connection with May Day celebrations dating back to pagan times:

> Persons convicted of having danced publicly on the first day of May are to be suspended from participating in the Holy Communion without being warned for the first offence, but publicly warned on a repetition of their sin.

Nothing remains, therefore, of the Jersey songs and dances that existed before the Reformation.

Lawrence Stone's twentieth-century comments about the effects of the Reformation as a whole are also applicable to what happened in Jersey. It:

> destroyed the social and psychological supports upon which both the community and the individual had depended for comfort and to give symbolic meaning to their existence . . . Man now stood alone before his Maker, with nothing but his conscience, the Bible and the preachers to guide him, deprived

of all the old psychological props, collective rituals, and opportunities for blowing off steam.

And certainly there were examples in Jersey of Islanders looking for ways of 'blowing off steam'. Mischief under cover of dark was much favoured. It could take the simple form of howling like a dog to disturb the sleeping neighbourhood, or of 'borrowing' a farmer's horse for a night ride round the countryside.

The mischief, though, could be even more daring – wild night revels. In 1699 these had grown to such proportions that an Act was passed which stated: 'Whereas large gangs masked and carrying clubs, career at night from house to house committing innumerable obscenities and enormities, the police are ordered to arrest all-night revellers, that they may receive exemplary punishment.'

Still the revels did not stop, for in 1619 Catherine Le Sauteur was 'convicted of joining in night revels, dressed as a man and wearing breeches'. So outrageous and morally unacceptable was her behaviour deemed, that she was put in the stocks two days running. On the Saturday she had to sit in the midst of the market crowds in St Helier with her shameful breeches hung beside her: on the Sunday she was set up as an example in the stocks outside St Peter's Church.

However, the reaction against the strict discipline of the Church and State, which attempted to stamp out idolatory and loose living, was not always as innocent as night revels. Some Islanders turned against Calvinism in favour of superstitions more sinister than any of the Catholic practices had ever been. They turned to witchcraft.

Witches

*T*he outsider, the one who dares to be different, has always been mistrusted. When crops fail or children die unexpectedly, the blame has to be laid at somebody's door. But it must be admitted, too, that being the member of a secret, anti-establishment society has always held a great attraction for some – young and old – men and women.

The power that a witch is supposed to have – be he eccentric, scapegoat or member of a secret cult, is called 'magic'. As Freud observes: 'Magic has to serve the most varied purposes – it must subject natural phenomena to the will of man, it must protect the individual from his enemies and from dangers and it must give him power to injure his enemies.' Freud concludes, therefore, that 'it is easy to perceive the motives which lead men to practise magic: they are human wishes.'

When it comes to Jersey witches, G.R. Balleine – whose work on the subject in the 1930s is invaluable – is in no doubt as to which category they belong. 'In the sixteenth and seventeenth centuries all the Governments of Western Europe, Catholic and Protestant alike, were fighting a fanatical secret society.' This secret society had the Devil as its god and parodies of Christian Sacraments as its rituals.

Balleine also believed that it was a cult organised on international lines. Its travelling ministry gave the same instructions to every coven, whatever their country – whether it practised in Pendle Forest, in Brittany, in the Orkneys, Sweden or here, in Jersey. For witch trials all over Europe have revealed that the organisation was always the same. When Mussorgsky wrote his 'St John's Night on the Bare Mountain' in 1867, he was describing in musical terms the almost identical rites that used to be practised by witches in his native Russia.

Each coven, or committee running the local branch of the society, had to have thirteen members. The President of the Sabbat, or meeting, which was usually held on a Friday, was always a man previously unknown in the locality. He was believed to be the Devil himself and, to lead the rituals, dressed himself in skins and covered his head with a mask, usually of a horned animal such as a bull, goat or stag. Homage was paid to him by kissing his backside. All new converts he stamped or tattooed with an indelible secret mark – 'la merche du diable'.

How did such a secret society come into being? Why did it grow to such proportions in the Europe of the sixteenth and seventeenth centuries in particular? There are two theories. One is that the pagan rites, which the Catholic Church tried so hard to eradicate, were never quite wiped out. They merely went underground but, ironically, because of Catholic influence, the old pagan gods were now worshipped as devils. Another theory is that Devil worship was one of the many heresies that flourished in the Middle Ages.

Whatever the origin of Devil worship and its attendant witchcraft, it obviously took advantage of the schisms in the established Catholic Church and came to the height of its power at the time of the Reformation and its aftermath.

In Jersey, though there were witch trials right through the reigns of Elizabeth I, James I, Charles I and during the Civil War, they began to be held in ever-increasing numbers while the Island was in the grip of Calvinism. The years from 1548 to 1620 were a time of theocracy, when Church and State combined to keep the community in God's favour. They attempted this by austere discipline, hard work, much prayer and abstinence from what they considered 'lewd' amusements.

Anyone who deviated from Calvin's strict code of conduct was considered to be in the pay of the Devil and, therefore, a threat to God himself. For the sake of the Island's good government and the spiritual well-being of its population, all such deviants – such as witches – had to be hunted out and destroyed.

There is no doubt, therefore, that both civil and ecclesiastical authorities, as well as the common people of Jersey, believed most definitely in witches and their power to subvert. It was a strong and long-lasting belief that manifested itself in superstitions as well as inhumane ways of stamping out the evil. The utilitarian stones, for example, which jutted from old granite chimneys to prevent seepage of rain-water under thatched roofs were known as 'witches' stones'. It was thought they were used by witches as resting-places on their flights over the Island on their broomsticks.

To guard against the evil power of witches, families often had crosses engraved on the chamfer stops of doors, windows and fireplaces – any place where they might gain dreaded entrance. An acorn carried about in one's pocket, or carved somewhere in the house, was also a recognised talisman against their 'evil eye'.

Nou dit qui l'est chorchi car il a bague souos l'yi.
'He is said to be a sorcerer because he has rings under his eyes.'

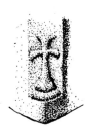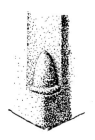

J. Stevens

What They Did

There is some evidence in the trials that Balleine has selected to show that at least some of the men and women were part of a special sect, with rites and ceremonies of their own at their Sabbats. From various testimonies, given both here and in Guernsey, the proceedings at their meetings seemed to follow a set pattern. First of all there would be the introduction of the convert and the initiation rites. One Guernsey witch gave evidence at her trial that the Devil appeared at the Sabbat as a dog with two great horns sticking up, and 'with one of his paws, which seemed like hands, he took her by the hand and told her she was welcome'.

So once converts to this secret society had been introduced to the coven and its President, kissed the Devil's backside, received his mark and sealed the pact with a few drops of blood, even a finger joint, what else did they do? One of the rituals was a parody of the Holy Communion Service conducted by the Devil. At her trial in 1617, Collette du Mont of St Saviour, Guernsey, described how this was done in her coven; 'The Devil poured black wine out of a wooden bowl, but it was not so good.' All present were called upon to renounce the Trinity of God the Father, Son and Holy Ghost and worship only the Devil. They were to pray to the Devil in the words 'Our Great Master, help us.'

Another of the activities – which gave more than usual pleasure, as it was frowned upon in their everyday lives – was dancing. There were three different formation dances for them to take part in. One involved dancing back to back, another was a long chain-dance, in which the Devil himself took the part of leader. The third was a circle dance during which the dancers whirled round and round a rock on which the Devil sat in his disguise of cat or crow or some horned animal.

One Guernsey witch said that at their meetings the dance was led by a black cat, that one of the women present gave it the ritual kiss on its behind, while the others knelt in front of it in worship. She went on to confess that 'they assembled before the said cat four times a week, and they adored the said cat, and the cat gave them dark bread which he bade them eat'.

Whether there were hallucinatory drugs in what they ate or drank at these midnight orgies is not known. Some authorities believe that the black ointment with which they were supposed to cover themselves at these meetings may have had hallucinogenic properties. The recipe for such a black ointment can be found in Scott's *Discoverie of Witchcraft* (1584). They were supposed to take:

The fat of young children, and seeth it with water in a brazen vessell, reserving the thickest of that which remaineth boiled, at the bottom, which they lay up and keep until occasion serveth to use it. They put hereunto Eleoselinum, Aconitum, Belladonna, Soote and Solanum Somniferum. They mix all these together, and they rub all parts of their bodies exceedingly till they look red, and be very hot, so as the pores may be opened, and their flesh soluble and loose. They join herewithal, either fat or oil, so that the force of the ointment may pierce inward and so be more effectual. By this means, on a moonlight night, they seem to be carried in the air to feastings, singings, dancings, kissings, em bracings, and other acts.

Whatever the source of their belief, many of those who attended these witches' meetings did believe that they had supernatural powers. Many, therefore, were convinced that they did indeed ride through the night to practise their black art. Collette du Mont, for example, declared at her trial in 1617 that, after she had rubbed herself back and front with some special powder and then walked out of her house, she was straight away wafted through the air and landed almost immediately at the place of the Sabbat.

The black art they practised – often carefully planned at the Sabbat – ranged from merely annoying the neighbours to actually causing their death. As most of the population were in farming, the evidence given at the trials suggests that the witch's magic was mostly directed against livestock – particularly cows. A farmer would find that his cow's milk had curdled, or that it had blood in it, or that it had dried up alto-gether. Sometimes the cows would be poisoned and die.

Other practices attributed to witches were the displacement of boundary stones; the removal of furze bundles at gateways to keep the sheep from straying from the hillside field. More personal and, therefore, more terrifying, was the sudden appearance in a bed of a 'sorceret'. These 'spells' made up of feathers and pieces of flax or wool twisted into the shape of cushions or apples, were to alert the victim that he was being bewitched.

By far the most frightening power the witches had, though, was that of suggestion. Balleine calls it the opposite of faith-healing – faith-killing. Witches traded on the psychological fact that if a man was told he would die, his self-confidence in staying alive would be so undermined that in many cases he would indeed die. Pasquette Le Vesconte, who had already once been tried as a witch and banished from Jersey, confessed in 1585 that 'she had entered into partnership with the Devil, and by his help perpetrated innumerable crimes and homicides'.

> *Méfie té des chorciers et touone ta paûte a l'envers.*
> *Beware of sorcerers and turn your pocket inside out*

Testing for a Witch

To hunt out these 'good-for-nothing, vicious and pernicious members of society', harsh methods were certainly employed. Nevertheless, because witchcraft was an offence punishable by death, the court procedure of the witch trials in Jersey was strictly laid down and for those days surprisingly fair.

If anyone was suspected of being a witch, she (it was three times more likely for a witch to be a woman than a man) was first taken before the Parish Constable and an informal jury of six. If these seven decided that there was a case to answer, that the accused seemed to be 'plutot coupable qu' innocent' – more guilty than innocent – she was then sent before the Bailiff and three Jurats.

Here, at the Cour de Cattel, she was asked whether she would submit her case to a jury of twenty-four landowners – eight from her own and eight from each of the adjoining parishes – the Grand Enquête du Pays. She was absolutely free to say 'yes' or 'no'. If 'yes', she was sent to Gorey Castle, Mont Orgueil, to wait for the next court sitting.

When her case came up, the jury was chosen by the Attorney General but, if the prisoner thought that any member might be prejudiced against her, she was free to challenge his inclusion. After the hearing of the evidence against the accused (and in the trial of Marie Grandin in 1648 there were between seventy and eighty witnesses to testify to her guilt) the verdict, if 'guilty', had to be agreed by at least twenty of the twenty-four jurors. For at least five jurors to bring in a verdict of 'not guilty' was enough to secure an acquittal.

There were cases when, for whatever reason, the accused refused to be tried by the Grand Enquête du Pays. In those cases there was nothing for the Bailiff to do but send her back to Gorey Castle, where it was hoped she would change her mind.

There is no evidence to show that torture was used in any part of these proceedings, either to extort a confession, or to make the accused give away accomplices. The same cannot be said of the witch trials in Guernsey where the use of torture was normal practice. Many times the phrases 'having been put to the torture she confessed', or 'to make them reveal their accomplices it is ordered that they be tortured before being executed', are to be found in records of the Guernsey witch trials. Warburton in his *Treatise on the History, Laws and Customs of the Island of Guernsey* dated 1682 gives the brutal details:

Yet this practice of torturing does not appear to have been used in the island for some ages, except in the case of witches, when it was too frequently applied, near a century since. The custom then was, when any person was supposed guilty of sorcery or witchcraft, they carried them to a place in the town called La Tour Beauregard, and there, tying their hands behind them by the two thumbs, drew them to a certain height with an engine made for that purpose, by which means sometimes their shoulders were turned round, and sometimes their thumbs torn off; but this fancy of witches has for some years been laid aside.

Once a witch had been charged, it was then that any justice in the actual court procedure of the trial was all too often cancelled out by the hysterical and superstitious content of the evidence given and, incredibly, accepted. There were, for example, certain characteristics that were thought to be indisputable proof of a witch's guilt. The mark of the Devil had to be searched for first. This was thought to appear either as a blue spot, or in the shape of a hare or toad, somewhere on the body. In those witch-hunting times it was not unusual for a birthmark to be taken for 'la merche du diable'.

Other sure signs of someone being a witch were an insensibility to shed tears and an ability to be pricked without shedding blood. That the carrying out of a pricking test could be particularly unpleasant and degrading can be seen from the procedure of a professional, Scottish witch-hunter in Newcastle, who sought to prove that the woman he had hauled before the court was indeed 'a child of the devil':

> The said witch-finder acquainted Lieutenant-Colonel Hobson that he knew women whether they were witches or no by their looks; and when the said person was searching of a personable and good-like woman, the said colonel replied and said, 'Surely this woman is none, and need not be tried;' but the Scotchman said she was, for the town said she was, and therefore he would try her; and presently, in sight of all the people, laid her body naked to the waist, with her clothes over her head by which fright and shame all her blood contracted into one part of her body, and then he ran a pin into her thigh, and then suddenly

let her coats fall, and then demanded whether she had nothing of his in her body, but did not bleed? But she, being amazed, replied little. Then he put his hands up her coats and pulled out the pin, and set her aside as a guilty person and child of the devil, and fell to try others, whom he made guilty. Lieutenant Colonel Hobson, perceiving the alteration of the aforesaid woman by her blood settling in her right parts, caused that woman to be brought again, and her clothes pulled up to her thigh, and required the Scot to run the pin into the same place, and

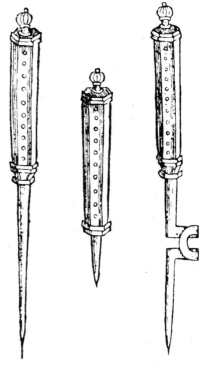

then it gushed out of blood, and the said Scot cleared her, and said she was not a child of the devil.

A second test for proving a suspect innocent or guilty was the water test. The accused witch was thrown into deep water – if she floated, she was obviously guilty: if she sank to the bottom, she was innocent – and often drowned. Whether the water test was used in Jersey or not, the pricking test certainly was.

Witch Trials in the Sixteenth and Seventeenth Centuries

It should be remembered that 300 to 400 years ago even to steal anything worth more than a shilling was a hanging offence. It also seems that most judges trying witches in the sixteenth and seventeenth centuries in Jersey appeared to presume the accused guilty until proved innocent. Yet, in the sixty-six witch trials selected for analysis by Balleine from the many witch trials held between 1562 and 1736, the number of people who were condemned to die as proven witches was only thirty-three.

Of the other thirty-three accused, eight were banished from Jersey, twelve were released with a severe warning as to their future conduct, five were completely acquitted, two died before they could be tried, while the fate of the other six is unknown. In those corruptible days, the prison wardens could have been bribed to effect an escape, or perhaps some of those six also died in the Castle before their cases could be heard.

Of the five witch trials held in November and December of 1585 that Balleine selects, all ended in the death-penalty. The judgement given in the case of one of them, Jean Mourant, is interesting in that it not only includes the sentence meted out but also the confession of the accused:

> Jean Mourant having been so forgetful of his salvation as to make a contract with the Devil, confessed with his own mouth his dealings with the Devil by mark and pact, confirmed by pledge and gift of one of his limbs, by means of which he had committed infinite mischiefs, crimes and homicides by reason of which he has been condemned as a criminal to be strangled until he is dead and his body burnt until it is entirely consumed and to have all his goods and chattels confiscated.

The idea that the body of a witch had to be burnt can be traced back to the age-old belief that fire had the property to purify. It also prevented the body having an honourable burial. In Jersey that savage sentence was somewhat modified, in that all the witches were ordered to be strangled before their bodies were cast into the flames.

In Guernsey the Courts were not so merciful. They often ordered a witch to be tied to a stake and burnt alive. To what lengths the Guernsey authorities were prepared to go in seeing that a sentence was carried out to the last letter can be judged from the following brutal tale.

In 1556, in Mary Tudor's Catholic reign, Katherine Gowches and her two daughters from St Peter Port did not attend church as they should have done. When this fact was brought to the attention of the Dean, as well as bringing up the subject of non-attendance at church, he questioned them about the sacrament of the altar. Their answers made him declare them heretics, though the women claimed that their answers were what they were taught in the previous reign of Edward VI. Their offer to change their beliefs to suit Mary Tudor did not affect the Bailiff's decision to burn them.

When the three women were committed alive to the flames, one of the daughters began to give birth to a baby boy. Seeing that the innocent child was about to be burned, too, one of the bystanders rescued it from the flames. The Bailiff, adamant that anything to do with the three heretics had to be destroyed, ordered the bystander to throw the baby back into the flames. For those watching there was an added horror perhaps not appreciated today. The Catholic Church taught that unbaptised infants burnt eternally in hell. Tennyson recaptures the monstrous moment in his play 'Queen Mary':

> *Sir, in Guernsey*
> *I watched a woman burn; and in her agony*
> *The mother came upon her – a child was born –*
> *And, Sir, they hurl'd it back into the fire,*
> *That, being thus baptised in fire, the babe*
> *Might be in fire forever. Ah, good neighbour,*
> *There should be something fiercer than fire*
> *To yield them their deserts.*

Some of the witches attracted more morbid interest to their activities, their trials and their eventual executions than others. The spectacle of their deaths was one of the few excitements that an Islander could expect in his drab existence. Mary Esnouf was one of these, more especially because she was none other than the grand daughter of a former Rector of St John. The record of the 1648 trial shows not only a large number of witnesses – over sixty – testifying that she had been guilty of 'divers diabolical things', but also gives details of the search made on her for the Devil's mark.

She was shaved by a surgeon and when no mark was found on her body she was ordered to open her mouth. In there, on her palate, the

Devil's mark was at last located. Then she was pricked with a lancet, but stated that she felt no pain. These two signs and the written allegations of the witnesses were enough to convict her – she was sentenced to be hanged and then strangled and then burned in the Market Place.

The Burning of Katherine Caviches, and her two Daughters in the Isle of Guernsey.

According to a chronicle of the time, there were even more people in St Helier to see her die than there had been when Prince Charles had visited Jersey during his exile. Men, women and children crowded on to the churchyard walls and up the slopes of Town Hill to witness her death as a witch in what is now the Royal Square.

Another witch who made a great impression on Islanders – one which has lasted into the present century – was Mary Tourgis. She came from a bad family – her mother was executed as a witch – and she herself first appeared in front of the Court in 1608. Perhaps because of her youth, she was then acquitted and was put into the Hulvet family as a domestic servant. They were to report to the Court if she misbehaved.

Ten years later Marie Tourgis was before the Court again. She was accused of 'many abominable deeds, wrought by the diabolic art of witchcraft, and having confessed that she had caused the death of a child, and bewitched a woman, she was condemned to go to the ordinary place of execution, and there hanged and strangled till death ensued, and her body reduced to ashes'.

The memory of such a seemingly powerful witch is kept alive in the saying still sometimes heard in the east of the Island. 'Si tais si maychante, j'enviethai cherchi Marie Tourgis.' (If you're such a wicked child, I'll send for Marie Tourgis.)

Three of the women tried between 1583 and 1649 show what different fates awaited those who had been charged with witchcraft. Marion Corbel was unfortunate enough to die in Gorey Castle before the evidence brought against her could be heard. Rather naturally, as she had not been convicted of any crime before her death, her family claimed that her property should not have been confiscated by the Crown but given to her heirs. In a famous, often-quoted, decision, the Court counter-claimed that an owner's death did not prevent the forfeiture of property incurred by the committing of a crime. So Marion Corbel's heirs came away empty-handed.

Then there was the obstinate Perrine Alexandre. She was kept a prisoner in Gorey Castle for a whole year on nothing but bread and water because she refused to agree to trial by Enquête. She was so adamant in her refusal that the authorities were left with no choice. They were at last forced to release her – with a warning.

Perhaps Guillemete du Vaistain suffered the worst fate of the three. She was a native of Normandy, as well as being the mother of Thomasse Le Ruez. This daughter had been one of the seven tried in the notorious witch trials of 1648. Before Guillemete du Vaistain was banished from Jersey – 'to purge the island of such dangerous and worthless persons' – she was flogged.

> *Grandes ouotheilles et p'tit bé,*
> *Ou n'éthaie jamais faim ni sé.*
> *Grand bé et p'tites ouotheilles*
> *Vos flanquethont vite au Vier Châté.*
> *Large ears and little mouth,*
> *From hunger and thirst will keep you.*
> *Large mouth and little ears*
> *In the old castle will fling you.*

The Witches' Clients

It was not just the witches themselves that so worried the Jersey authorities – it was also those who sought their aid. In those doctorless, vetless days, when the usual herbal remedies had failed them or their livestock, Islanders would often turn to a witch in the last desperate hope of a cure.

Jeanne Le Vesconte was one of the many tried and executed at the end of 1585. Her formal sentence is as follows:

> Whereas common report has long suspected Jeanne Le Vesconte of the diabolical art of Witchcraft, charging her with constantly using spells and wicked devices, sometimes against people, sometimes against their goods, making some ill, and curing others; and whereas complaints and scandals have so multiplied, that she has been arrested; she has voluntarily submitted the question of her guilt or innocence, her life or death, to an Enquête du Pays. The said Enquête of twenty-four, having been sworn and purged of suspicion, as custom requires, has unanimously voted for her condemnation to death; according to which verdict she is sentenced to be hanged, till death ensues, and in detestation of her crime to be reduced to ashes, and all her goods, chattels, and property confiscated to the Crown or the Seigneur to whom it belongs. Whereupon the Procureur of Sir Philippe de Carteret, Seigneur of St. Ouen, has demanded that the execution shall take place on the Fief of the said Seigneur, and this claim has been allowed in virtue of the fact that he has the right of High Justice, and that she was one of the tenants of the manor. The Viscount is to see this sentence carried out.

Not only is it interesting that the Seigneur of St Ouen demanded that the execution should take place in his fief – because he then had the right to confiscate the witch's property – but that Jeanne Le Vesconte is accused of 'curing' people as well as 'making some ill'.

Then, in the same year there was the case of the Le Brocq family. Jacque Le Brocq's daughter fell ill and so two of the family were sent to a woman, suspected of being a witch, for something to cure her. For doing such 'an abominable thing' and one which 'contravenes the ordinances and commandments of God', the two who had sought the witch out and the father who had sent them, were, all three, detained in Gorey Castle.

In 1591 it was recorded 'Whereas Jean Bichard has had recourse to a sorcerer for an injury to his leg, a wicked thing to do, and one expressly forbidden by the laws of God, and the ordinances of His Justice; he is hereby condemned to be placed in the stocks on Sunday in the Parish of St Peter.'

To prevent any further trafficking with witches, in 1591 the Royal Court passed the following Ordinance:

'This Act declares that for the time to come everyone shall turn away from such iniquitous and diabolical practices, against which the law of God decrees the same punishments as against Witches and Enchanters themselves; and also in order that the Divine Vengeance may be averted, which on account of the impurity with which these crimes have been committed, now threatens those who have the repression of them in their hands. It is, therefore, strictly forbidden to all the inhabitants of this island to receive any counsel or assistance in their adversities from any Witches or Diviners, or anyone suspected of practicing Sorcery, under pain of one month's imprisonment in the castle on bread and water; and on their liberation they shall declare to the Court the cause of such presumption, and according as this shall appear reasonable, shall be dealt with as the law of God directs.'

Witches in the Family

Did the family or parish into which an Islander was born shorten the odds for growing up to be a witch? Balleine's analysis would suggest it did. More witches, for example, seemed to come from St Ouen and St Martin than from St Brelade or Trinity. St Clement was particularly feared as a centre of witchcraft, with its focus the forty foot-high granite rock standing on Le Nez point, known as Rocqueberg. Its top vitrified by lightning and a ledge half-way down seeming to have the imprint of the cloven hoof of the Devil himself, it was an ideal rendezvous for practitioners in the Black Art. Now the rock is in a private garden, but

400 years ago it must have been one of the most desolate spots in Jersey.

All five from Balleine's list who were charged in St Clement were found to be guilty of witchcraft and executed. Jean Mourant was tried in 1585, Collette Horman, Ysic Hardyne and Germaine Royal were all tried in October 1611, and the fifth, Marie Filleul, tried in 1625, was hanged at Samares Manor on the Seigneur's own gallows – as he insisted was right and proper – because she lived in his fief. Just as when the Seigneur of St Ouen had claimed his grisly right in the case of Jeanne Le Vesconte, this meant that the Seigneur of Samares would also have the power to confiscate all Marie Filleul's goods and property.

When it came to witchcraft running in families, both the Alexandres and the Grandins had five members of their family tried as witches. In the case of the Grandins, in 1606, when Marie and Elizabeth Grandin could only have been young girls, they were arrested as witches. As the jury could not agree on their guilt, they were released with a warning. They were 'not to gad about the island, nor to threaten or speak evil of anyone, under pain of being rearrested and punished for the crime with which they had been charged'. Then the Bailiff gave them advice 'to walk in the fear of God, to attend Divine Service regularly, to live in peace and concord with their neighbours, and to labour faithfully to earn their own living, and so by honest and upright conduct to gain such a good character that their bad reputation would be forgotten'.

The records then show that in 1631 a Jeanne Grandin was hanged and burnt as a witch and that in 1648, forty-two years after her first trial, Elizabeth was again before the Court. She was accused of living 'a lewd, wicked and scandalous life', and once more urged to live in the fear of God, not to slander or speak ill of her neighbours, nor to 'unstop the côtils', or she would be banished from Jersey. Her illegitimate daughter, Marie, was also arrested and warned to be of good behaviour.

The story of the third Marie Grandin is a sad one, because right to the very end she persisted in her claim that she was innocent. The charge against her was that she had 'by diabolical spells caused many persons to die, and others to fall into a decline, and also much cattle', and there were between seventy and eighty witnesses to testify that the charge against her was justified. More than that, when in prison her head had been shaved and examined by surgeons and a mark was found. As this mark, when pricked, bled on one side and not on the other, it proved itself to be the dread 'merche du diable'.

The verdict of 'guilty' was, therefore, unanimous. She was condemned to be led to the stake in the market-place, with the rope to kill her already hanging round her neck, there to be strangled and her body burned. She was just one of the seven women who were executed as witches in the notorious year of 1648.

Evidence taken against Collas Becquet when she was tried as a witch in Guernsey:

Depositions Against Collas Becquet. May 17, 1617

Susanne Le Tellier, widow of *Pierre Rougier*, deposed that after her husband was dead she found witches' spells in his bed; and that while he was upon his said deathbed he complained of being bewitched by *Collas Becquet*, with whom he had had a quarrel, and who during the quarrel told him he would repent of it; whereupon he was taken with ..*, whereof he was ill for twelve days; they also found forty four witches' spells in her child's pillow, some of which were made like hedgehogs, others round like apples, and others again flat like the palm of the hand; and they were of hempen thread twisted with feathers.

Susanne, wife of *Jean Le Messurier*, deposed that her husband and *Collas Becquet* had angry words together one day; they had an infant about six weeks old, and as she was undressing it in the evening to put it to bed, there fell upon the stomach of the said infant, a black beast which melted away as soon as it fell, so that although she carefully sought for it, she could never discover what had become of it; immediately afterwards the infant was taken ill and would not suck, but was much tormented; being advised to look into the said infant's pillow, she found there several witches' spells sewn with thread; these she took out and carefully dressed all the feathers in the pillow;

yet when she examined it again a week afterwards, she found there a black bean with a hole in it; of which, the said *Becquet* hearing that he was suspected, his wife came to witness's house while the said *Becquet* was at sea, and told her that on account of the rumour which witness had raised about her husband, he the said *Becquet* would thrash the said *Messurier*, her husband, and herself, and would kill them; after that, witness went to their house to say they were not afraid either of him or her, or of their threats to kill her husband and her; witness had six big chickens which ran after their mother, going out of the house in the morning and returning at night; and one by one they began to jump up against the chimney and eat the soot, so that they all died one after the other, ... * as they jumped, until the last one which remained alive up to one hour of daybreak, when it died; after they had told this to Mr. *de Lisle*, and he had threatened the people, her infant recovered and remained well.

Collas Rougier deposed that his brother *Pierre Rougier* when dying charged *Collas Becquet* with causing his death.

Collas Hugues reported that being at a wedding, *Collas Becquet* arrived there, and began to toy with his daughter-in-law, who repelled his advances; the very same evening she was taken ill in such a manner that they thought she would have died from one hour to another; besides which she remained under the charm, and they found one of the witches' spells in her bed, which was shown to the Members of the Court, who were making an inspection at St Peter's; the said girl sometimes fell to the ground quite blinded.

The wife of the said *Hugues* deposed to exactly the same as her husband.

Jean de Garis, son of *William*, deposed that about two or three years ago, having lent some money on pledge to *Collas Becquet*, he asked him for money, or else for a verification of his security; when the said *Becquet* replied that he would let him know what his security was; the said *de Garis* having then returned home, found his daughter sick and afflicted; they found witches' spells and other conjurations several times in their child's pillow; but the mother of the said *Becquet* having come to the said *de Garis*'s house, he gave her a drink of water and half-a-loaf of bread, as he had been advised to do; since which time they had found nothing more in the child's pillow; however to avoid all risk of the said witches' spells they had always believed that this evil had come upon them by their means.

Mr. Thomas de Lisle deposed that *Thomas Brouart*, who resided in his house, having called the son of *Collas Becquet* a wizard, it happened that there was one day found in the said Thomas's bed a great number of maggots, which the said *Sieur de Lisle* saw, and compared to an ant-hill, so lively and thick were they, and they could hardly clear the said child of them, although they put it in different places; afterwards the said child gathered lice in such a manner that although its shirts and clothes were changed every day they could not free it; the said *Thomas Brouart* also had a brand new vest, which was so covered with lice that it was impossible to see the cloth, and he was compelled to have it thrown among the cabbages; upon which he went and threatened *Massi*'s wife that he would beat her if she did not abstain from thus treating his child; and on returning he found the said vest among the cabbages clear of lice, which had also since then quitted the said *Brouart*.

Jacques le Mesurier deposed that about two or three years ago he met *Collas Becquet* and *Perot Massi*, who had some fish and who moreover owed him money; he wished to take some of their fish at a reduced price, but they would not agree to it, and they quarrelled; whereupon one of the two, either *Becquet* or *Massi*, threatened him that he would repent of it; and at the end of two or three days, he was seized with a sickness in which he first burnt like fire and then was benumbed with cold so that nothing would warm him, and this without any cessation; he suffered in this way for nearly a month. *Collas Becquet* heard that witness charged him with being the cause of his sickness, and he threatened that he would kill witness; but very soon afterwards the said witness was cured; and he affirms and believes that the said *Becquet* and *Massy*, or one of them, was the cause of his attack.

Note on the Guernsey Records

The Records at the Guernsey *Greffe*, from which the foregoing confessions and depositions have been transcribed, and whence the following list of accusations is compiled, are of a very voluminous character. In fact there is enough matter in them, connected with witchcraft alone, to fill at least a couple of thick octavo volumes. There is, however, so much sameness in the different cases, and such a common tradition running through the whole, that the present excerpts give a very fair idea of the features which characterise the mass. While some of these records are tolerably complete, the greater part of them unfortunately are fragmentary and imperfect. The books in which they were originally written seem to have been formed of a few sheets of paper stitched together. Then at some later period a number of these separate sections – in a more or less tattered condition – were gathered into volumes and bound together in vellum. It is evident, however, that very little care was exercised in their arrangement in chronological order. The consequence is that one portion of a trial sometimes occurs in one part of a volume, and the rest in another part; sometimes the depositions alone seem to have been preserved; sometimes the confessions; while in many cases the sentences pronounced are all that can now be discovered. Nevertheless these old records enshrine much that is interesting, and very well deserve a more exhaustive analysis than they have ever yet received. There are also in the margins of these volumes, scores of pen-and-ink sketches of a most primitive description, depicting the carrying out of the various rigours of the law. Rough and uncouth as these illustrations are, they nevertheless possess a good deal of graphic significance …. They represent, for instance, culprits hanging on the gallows – sometimes two or three in a row – with a fire kindled underneath; others attached to stakes in the midst of the flames; others, again, racing away under the lash of the executioner, &c., &c., and thus form a most realistic comment on the judicial severities recorded in the text.

Extract taken from J. Pitts *Witchcraft and Devil Lore in the Channel Islands.*

A Hindsight View of the Jersey Witch Trials

The theory that witchcraft in Jersey was part of a European secret society, and that the majority of those tried were indeed attempting to subvert the Island's institutions, is tenable. But there is another possibility – that the whole witchcraft phenomenon in Jersey was generated by suppression and mass hysteria.

With normal outlets for relaxation and enjoyment strictly forbidden, is it any wonder that many admitted in their confessions that they found great pleasure in their midnight Sabbats? The declarations of two girls in their twenties are typical: Jean Dibasson said the Sabbat was 'a veritable Paradise where one had greater pleasure than could be expressed'. Marie de la Ralde asserted that she saw no harm in going to the Sabbat, for she found more joy and contentment there than going to Mass, 'because the Devil was the true God.'

The notorious Salem witch trials in Massachusetts at the end of the seventeenth century prove only too well what can happen when civil and Church authorities act out of fear rather than with justice. Is it a coincidence that there was a close connection between Jersey and Salem from the latter's foundation in 1629? The early town records certainly abound in Jersey names.

Philip Le Geyt, Lieutenant-Bailiff from 1676 to 1715, was in no doubt as to the proper view of the witch trials. He wrote:

As Holy Scripture forbids us to allow witches to live, many persons have made it a matter of conscience and of religion to be severe in respect of such a crime. This principle has without doubt made many persons credulous. How often have purely accidental associations been taken as convincing proofs? How many innocent people have perished in the flames on the asserted testimony of supernatural circumstances? I will not say there are no witches; but ever since the difficulty of convicting them has been recognised in the island, they all seem to have disappeared, as though the evidence of the times gone by had been but an illusion. This shows the instability of all things here below.

Quant les filles sufflent le djiable s'ehuque.
When girls whistle the devil laughs outright.

Later Legends and Tales of Witchcraft

Only fifty-two years after the many executions in 1648, Balleine believed that the organised worship of the Devil as an alternative religion in Europe was virtually over. During the 200 years or so of its existence, the judicial murders for witchcraft in England alone are estimated at 30,000. In Guernsey, over more or less the same period, at least a hundred witches were tried, in Jersey even more. But by no means did that signify the end of witchcraft in Jersey. With the spread of literacy, books of magic could take over from the Presidents of the Covens in the dissemination of spells and charms.

A particularly popular book, printed in Cologne in 1722, was *Les Secrets Merveilleux de la Magic Naturelle et Cabalistique du Petit Albert*. This, and its companion, *The Grand Albert*, included recipes for love potions, charms, spells and cabalistic squares. *The Grand Albert* was known in Jersey as *Le Grand Mêle* and apparently this witches' Bible, once owned, could never be given or thrown away. However hard the owner tried to get rid of it, the book always appeared on the bookshelf again in the morning.

A typical charm would have been similar to this one, revealed at his trial by the notorious Provençal witch Bras-de-Fer: 'In a varnished earthen jar, which must neither have been bought nor obtained by barter, the blood of a sheep, wool, the hair of certain animals, and noxious herbs are mixed together, to an accompaniment of grimaces and superstitious ceremonies, and by invoking the demons with certain words.'

It was also something to be proud of in Jersey if there was anyone in the family who either clearly had *du scîn* – 'hidden knowledge', or boasted of having *le grand sang* – 'witch's blood' in their veins. For it was all too possible that an ancestress of theirs, in one of the midnight orgies in the sixteenth or seventeenth centuries, had indeed had intercourse with the 'Devil'.

In the eighteenth century it was the Ecclesiastical Court rather than the civic authorities who continued to clamp down heavily on any form of witchcraft as soon as it appeared. One extract from its Minute Book records the case against Marie Godfray, wife of Etienne Machon of St Saviour. She was accused in 1736 of 'dabbling in the Forbidden Arts and unveiling things that are hidden'. She then promised 'to abstain from such practices in the future, and moreover to disclose the names of any who approach her for this purpose. Neighbouring parishes are to be informed of this by the reading of this Act of the Court after the Nicene Creed.'

Fifty years later, in the *Gazette de Jersey* of 10 March 1787, there was an article complaining of a great increase of wizards and witches in the Island, as well as of their supposed victims. Of the 'ridiculous' scenes taking place, an example from St Brelade was cited...

A householder in that parish had dreamed that a wizard had come to him and ordered him to poison himself on a certain day but to tell no one of his suicide plan. Quite unable to keep such horrific information to himself, the poor man confided his dream to his wife.

Together they decided that the only course of action to take was to visit a white witch – *une Quéraude*. To overcome the evil spell of the wizard, the white witch suggested fasting first of all and then – on the day appointed for the suicide – a special ceremony.

For this ceremony the white witch, the husband and wife, together with four or five of their trusted friends, were to shut themselves up in a room. There they were to boil special herbs, roast a beeve's heart stuck full of nails and pins and read special passages from the Bible. All the time drawn swords were to be thrust up the chimney and down into the ground to prevent the black witch gaining entrance.

As the man survived the day, the white witch was paid well for her services, and, as apparently there were many others in St Brelade who also believed themselves bewitched, the white witches had a thriving and profitable trade in unbewitching them!

Rocqueberg

Certainly, too, a superstitious dread of Rocqueberg lingered on long after it was reputed to be the centre of sorcery in St Clement. A tourist guide as late as 1875 declares:

> No Jersey girl or Jersey man would have brought you here on a Friday night, particularly if there was a full moon. The Prince of Darkness has a special fancy for the locality. He frequently came here in former days and still manifests himself.

Not surprisingly, two legends have become associated with the rock. The first concerns the fisherman Hubert and his beautiful fiancée Madelaine. They were both happily awaiting the day when they would be man and wife, but the girl's happiness was clouded by her fiance's often abstracted behaviour. He was very attracted by sorcery and would wander about at night looking for super-natural happenings.

One night Hubert went on his usual nocturnal wanderings but this time in the direction of Rocqueberg Point. Feeling tired, he sat down near the rock to have a rest before the journey home. Then, suddenly, instead of the bleak promontory in front of him, there was a wooded glade, with enchanting, beautiful girls dancing in and out of the trees.

The most beautiful of the girls approached him and asked him to come with her and join in the revels. So enjoyable were they that, when his fair companion invited him to come again the following night, he accepted with alacrity.

Once home, the young fisherman just could not keep his adventure to himself – he told Madelaine. She was amazed at his tale but was even more astonished, when he told her that he had every intention of going to Rocqueberg the following night.

In her distress the young girl sought the help of the parish priest. He advised her to follow her young man wherever he went, but so that no harm should come to her, he handed her a large wooden crucifix.

Armed with this, the next night Madelaine followed the fisherman to Rocqueberg. To her horror, instead of a pleasant wooded glade and lovely girls disporting themselves round her fiance, she saw only the bleak rock and hideous old hags. They were shrieking and dancing round Hubert where he stood as if transfixed. So horrified was she by what she saw that she lifted the crucifix high into the air as if to ward off the ugly sight.

Immediately the old hags, with one last and piercing shriek, completely disappeared. At this terrifying sound, Hubert fell unconscious to the ground. Whether Hubert was a wiser man after he came round and whether he was suitably grateful to his courageous and beautiful Madelaine is not told.

The complete disappearance for ever of the witches of Rocqueberg from their bleak promontory belongs to another tale – again involving a fisherman.

These witches had decreed that if any fisherman passing their rock wanted to complete his journey in safety, then he had to throw to them, as tribute, the thirteenth fish he had caught. If he did not, then the witches would, by their singing of spells, raise such a storm that his boat would immediately be cast against the rock and utterly smashed. For his negligence the fisherman himself

Rocqueberg

..ould be drowned. If, on the other hand, he remembered his toll and faithfully put aside the thirteenth fish he had caught, then no matter how hard a storm might be blowing, he and his ship would reach shore safely.

One day, as a young fisherman was sailing home past Rocqueberg, he saw the witches dancing on its peak, shrieking out their spells and blasphemous songs. The fisherman, despite the number of fellow sailors who had been drowned at that very spot and the storm that was raging, only laughed.

Then he held up something in his hand – his toll – for the witches to see. It was a great five-rayed starfish. As he sailed past the rock, he swiftly cut off one of its rays and threw the rest of the fish with all his strength at the dancing, singing hags. As he threw his tribute, he shouted against the storm: 'La Crouée est mon passport' (The Cross is my passport).

The starfish landed on the rock, in the midst of the witches, in the shape of a cross. The storm immediately died down, the witches, with a shriek, vanished – never to be seen again.

The Evil Eye and the Jersey Cow

As is to be expected, there are many tales of the 'evil eye' being cast on one of the farmer's most valuable assets – his cows. There was even a special spell – 'Butyrum de armento' – to make the cow give blood instead of milk. Its antidote was to put a stone axe into the cow's drinking water. The following three stories show how the 'evil eye' was eventually averted from its victims.

The first concerns a farmer who was having trouble not with just one cow but the whole herd. Their milk yield was getting lower and lower despite all the tried remedies he dosed them with. Finally, two of his cows died.

Then the farmer came to the conclusion that his cows were not afflicted with any earthly disease but were the victims of some sorcery. So he planned to stay up one night and watch his cows, as they were tethered in the field, with his gun by his side.

Much to his surprise, from the field belonging to a farmer with whom he had recently quarrelled bounded an enormous black dog. The dog ran straight to the front of the cows, stood on its hind legs and slowly, very slowly at first, began to dance. Gradually, one by one, the cows too began to stand up on their hind legs and, following the dog's rhythm, also began to dance.

Then the dog began to dance faster and faster and by the end of half an hour the cows were so winded, trying to follow the dog's increasing tempo, that they fell down exhausted. The farmer, seeing what had happened, had the presence of mind to fire at the dog just before it bounded back to the next field. He hit it in the leg and it went howling off.

When he met his neighbour the next day, he had his arm in a sling, and the farmer had no more trouble with his cows!

The second story concerns a lady whose cow's rich milk was renowned throughout the parish. Among the neighbours who came to her at milking time with their jugs to be filled was a certain Maître Ph'lip. He always asked and paid for a quart of milk, but the lady had her suspicions that the jug he presented daily held considerably more than a quart.

Determined not to be imposed on any further, one day she

Jersey traditional dress and dairy ware

suggested to Maître Ph'lip that she take his jug to the dairy to be measured. Without any hesitation, Maître Ph'lip agreed and handed over the jug – her suspicions were confirmed.

But the next day, thinking to give Maître Ph'lip only a quart and not a drop more, when she came to milk her cow – the cow was dry. No matter how hard she tried, not a drop of milk would the cow yield. What is more, Maître Ph'lip did not turn up as he usually did.

So when by chance she met Maître Ph'lip that same afternoon, she came straight to the point and asked why he had not come for his milk. 'Ma fé, j'avais peux qu'on' n'en éthest pas assez pour vous même' – 'My faith, I was afraid you would not have enough for yourself' was the ironic reply.

Then it was that she realised she had no ordinary customer on her hands but a sorcerer. So she gave in, told Maître Ph'lip to come as usual the next day – with his own jug – and, from that moment, her cow gave its usual quantity of rich milk.

Cream rather than milk is the subject of the third story. A certain lady had refused to marry a neighbour and out of pique it seemed that he had cast a spell on her cream-making. Whatever method she used her milk just would not turn. So in desperation she sought the advice of a white witch as to how the spell could be lifted. To get her own back on the rejected suitor, she had, in her turn, to bewitch something that he had made – cider. From each of the five barrels of cider he had stored, she was to steal just one bottleful. On her return home she was to take some of the cream that had not turned and add it to one of the bottles. Immediately the whole barrel of cider from which that bottle had been taken would turn sour. If the neighbour did not unbewitch her cream after that, then she still had four more barrels she could affect in the same way.

The lady thanked the witch for her advice, crossed her palm with silver and returned home to put the counter-spell into practice. That night she stole to her neighbour's outhouse, filled the five bottles with his cider, one from each cask, and came home. Then she put a little of her bewitched cream into one of the bottles and waited to see what would happen.

Next morning when she began to churn, to her great joy the cream began to appear. She never did have to go to the lengths of turning all five barrels of her neighbour's cider sour!

J'é'thons d'l'orage car les vaques ne font que d'bueûler.
We shall have thunder for the cows do nothing but low.

Witches' Revenge

There are many tales told of how a witch had the power – if she felt herself slighted or insulted – of making her scoffer unable to eat bread. In Jersey there is the story of Edward and the 'Black Lady'.

When Edward was about fourteen, ignoring the warnings of his parents never to annoy the 'Black Lady' because she was reported to be a witch, he did just that. He shouted after her in the street, 'Here comes the old negress.'

The 'Black Lady' turned and, looking straight into his eyes, prophesied, 'It will be a fine day, my lad, before you eat any bread.' When the terrified Edward got home, he found that he could not get a morsel of bread past his lips.

So Edward grew up quite unable to eat bread for, despite the efforts of his parents to find the 'Black Lady' to remove the spell, she had left the parish and could not be found. By the time he was eighteen, he had become a very sick boy indeed and the doctor feared for his life.

Then suddenly, at three o'clock in the morning on the fourth anniversary of his meeting with the 'Black Lady', Edward jumped out of bed, raced downstairs to the kitchen, seized hold of a loaf of bread and greedily began to eat it. He had just got to the last crust of bread in the house, when his father came down into the kitchen and saw that the terrible spell had at last been lifted.

When the family doctor was told the astonishing news, he did not seem all that surprised. 'The "Black Lady", as you call her, died at three o'clock this morning and the spell must have died with her.'

The last two stories, both said to be true, as the others were, concern the detection of one witch and the terrible revenge taken by another. There were two girls both in love with the same man. To clear the way to have the man to herself, one girl told the other that before the month was over she would die – and she did.

The neighbours were very suspicious of the circumstances surrounding the death of the young girl, so they consulted a white witch. She told them to take the clothes belonging to the dead girl into her garden, to pile them into a heap and then beat them with sticks. As this was being done, they were told, the one who had caused her death would confess.

The neighbours did as they were told and, as they were beating the pile of the dead girl's clothes with their sticks, there was a cry from an upstairs window. They looked up and saw the young girl who had caused the death, cowering away as if she was being hit. When they went up to her she confessed the full story. Then instead of using their sticks on the pile of clothes, they used them on the dead girl's sorcerer and beat her out of the neighbourhood.

In the second story, Jean, a farmer in St Lawrence, had an important contract to sign the following Saturday at the Royal Court in St Helier. A day or so before he went, a tramp came to his farm to beg for a pot of cider. Jean told him to go away and stop bothering him. The tramp's reply was that Jean had a choice – either to give him the cider, or to lose the important contract. Unless the tramp got his cider, Jean would never get to the Royal Court. The tramp still did not get his cider.

Jean and his neighbours laughed at the idea of someone like the tramp uttering such a threat and, when Saturday arrived, there was Jean, all dressed in his Sunday best, ready for the walk to St Helier and the signing of the important contract which could make him richer by a few hundred pounds. The neighbours all wished him a good journey, as he set off on his profitable mission.

All went well until he reached the top of Mont Cochon. Then he began to feel a tickling discomfort, first around his neck, then on his face. So bad did the irritation become, that he tore off his collar to get relief. He saw to his horror that the collar in his hand was covered with lice; looking down he noticed that so were all his clothes. From head to foot he was alive with lice.

In great shame, and fearful lest anyone should spot him in such a frightful state, he immediately turned round for home, cutting across the fields and keeping well to the hedgerows. Once home, he was amazed to find that not a single louse remained. But, of course, by then it was too late to get to the Royal Court in St Helier for the signing of the contract. The tramp had been right – because he had not been given his pot of cider, Jean had lost his contract.

Though the *Jersey Argus* boasted, on 17 November 1835, that better education had put paid in Jersey to what they called 'this silly belief' in witches, only days before they had published the following incredible case that had come in front of the Royal Court on 7 November.

Three young men from Grouville had been charged with threatening to kill Molly Gallichan with a huge stick, while she was milking her cow.

From the evidence presented by the defending Advocate it would appear that the sister of two of the young men, Esther Aubin, had gone when she was ill to seek the help of Molly Gallichan who – without any qualifications – had set herself up as a doctor. As a result of this visit, the three young men thought Esther Aubin had been bewitched. Since they laid the blame for this sorcery on the witch Molly Gallichan, that was why the three had threatened her.

This case aroused so much interest in the readers of *The Argus*, that one of its contributors, who called himself 'Observer', regaled them with three more stories about witches – this time from St Clement's Parish:

In the parish lives a respectable farmer, who, with his family, is a staunch believer in witchcraft. Nothing happens amiss in his family circle of affairs, which is not attributed to 'un mauvais regard' or to the evil power of 'les mauvaises gens'. Are their cattle ill? Or their crops blighted? – they have incurred the displeasure of some wretches having 'du savoir'. Sometime since, their daughter, when about eighteen years old, was seized with a slow and wasting disorder – a species of consumption, though attended with symptoms which are not the usual accompaniments of a decline. She became languid, a lowness of spirits followed, with a feeling of uneasiness, or, as it seemed, of horror. All these symptoms alarmed her affectionate but superstitious parents. They concluded that she was 'tinse des mauvaises gens' [influenced by witches] and the remedy in that case, was to apply to a 'queraud' (or 'queraude' – a charmer), who might, by their arts free her from the afflicting powers of a ruthless witch. They applied, and the poor girl, contrary to her inclination (for she was the only one who disbelieved in witchcraft, and still more so that she was the victim of any spell) was dragged to the residence of one of these 'querauds' at the Dicq. There our lingering patient remained a full week, and was compelled to swallow the drugs and the compounds given to her by the old woman and to listen to her blasphemous invocations! But she became feebler and feebler; at the end of her probation, she was removed to the house of friends, where, in a few days afterwards, death seized her body, and spirit fled!

The second story told by 'Observer' is still more remarkable:

A young woman attended a Methodist service held in a room at St Clement's in the same vingtaine and same road as in the previous case. The preacher took for his text, 'And I shall deliver them.' The text was no sooner read than she began to sob, to weep, to mutter, and finally to exclaim in a moaning voice: 'Oh yes, I shall be delivered! I shall! I shall! Yes! I shall be delivered from them!!' She was immediately taken into an adjoining kitchen, where on being questioned as to her moaning, and from whom she expected to be delivered, she answered: 'From them.' 'From whom?', she was asked; 'From my tormentors,' she replied with fear; 'Don't you see them? Don't you see them? There! There! Oh there they are! Oh, dear! What shall I do ? They are going to kill me!' All this was said in an unearthly voice and at length she became so convulsed as to over-power two men who were holding her. She made an attempt to get some knives which she spotted in a drawer, with the intention, so she said, to employ them in self-defence against the horrid crew who were assaulting her. With the greatest of difficulty she was prevented from using them. Shortly after this, the scene became terrific in the extreme – the yells which rent the air, the tortures which she appeared to suffer, the lateness of the hour and the confusion which ensued, all added to shake the nerves of the most resolute of the spectators. After remaining some hours in this state of fearful excitement, she became exhausted and sank into a state of weakness – she was then carried home and gradually recovered.

A third instance of the belief in witchcraft was given by 'Observer' on 29 March 1836:

A young sick girl who was convinced that she was being bewitched had eventually to have attendants. On one occasion she struggled with three female attendants, shrieking: 'The witches are at Rocquebert, ('twas a Friday night, too) and they are calling me to go with them. Let me go! oh, let me go! – don't detain me! Now you say you don't believe in witchcraft, but don't you see them now! There! There! There they are!!'

'Observer' concluded this tale by noting that the young girl remained in this pitiful condition for about six weeks, during which time she was unable to sleep. Eventually, though, she did recover.

Those tales all took place in the 1830s. In the *St. Martin's Parish Magazine* of 1896, the Reverend Thomas Le Neveu tells three more tales of supposed spells and enchantments which happened even nearer to our own time:

I may here speak of facts with which I have been personally acquainted, and relating to persons who have long passed away. In the year 1845, there was, in a certain parish, a house and garden which had remained unlet for several years, and the owner became persuaded that this was owing to a spell or charm (un sort), which some evil-minded person had cast upon the said property. To remove this, a notorious quack, or witch-doctor, from St. Ouen was sent for, who proceeded to fill a bottle with the decoction of certain herbs, and, late on Saturday night, this bottle – with mysterious incantations uttered over it

– was buried in the garden, and the deluded owner assured that a tenant would now soon come forward! Nothing of the kind happened, however.

Some ten years later than the above occurrence, a well-to-do farmer in the same parish, who had for some time been in an indifferent state of health (caused by his intemperate habits), came to the conclusion that his next-door neighbour – a quiet, inoffensive market-gardener – had bewitched him. Hence, having enticed the unsuspecting fellow into an outbuilding, and shut the door upon him, the farmer savagely belaboured him with a heavy cart-whip, for his supposed misdeeds!

Yet another case, of so recent a date as 1871: An aged fisherman, in the extreme north of the Island, suffered from certain ailments, which he, too, believed were due to the witches' enchantments; and, each Sunday morning, for weeks, I have seen him drive in his cart to a 'witch doctor' living some eight miles away, in the vain hope of being cured by him, but, of course, he was bitterly disappointed.

> *Le nais m'pique, ch'est seigne de mort.*
> *My nose tickles, it's a sign of death.*

Witches in the Twentieth Century

If the inclination is to scoff at our too credulous nineteenth-century ancestors, these are two cuttings from the *Evening Post* of 1932:

> Dear Sir – Since coming to Jersey, I have been greatly surprised at the superstitions of some of the people here, who otherwise appear quite sane. They fully believe in witchcraft, spells, the evil eye, charms, etc.
>
> Aches, pains, or even simple warts, they must go to the charmer, who is generally some dirty old man or woman. As far as I can gather, the only thing he seems to charm from them is his fee.
>
> Now, if local preachers could only be induced to say a few words against this practice, I am sure it would soon disappear.
>
> Yours faithfully,
W. BUTLER
La Robeline, St. Ouen's.

A psychologist, aged 34, who went to Guernsey from Jersey, appeared before the Guernsey Police Court this morning on a charge of pretending to predict fortunes and to foretell the future (writes our correspondent).

One witness gave evidence that she asked the man to find her husband. He then 'saw' him in a crystal glass and said he was in Manchester.

Another witness said that she visited the fortune teller on police instructions and asked him to find her brother. She was told her brother was living and that it would be to her advantage to get into touch with him.

Actually her brother was dead.

In both cases money was paid to the psychologist.

The Defendant in taking the oath said 'I swear by Allah.' He denied having said that he saw the missing husband in a crystal glass.

Inspector Sculpher, after the charges had been proved, said that in Jersey the fortune teller had been sentenced to nine months' hard labour for 'black magic'. His history on the mainland could

*Witches bottles and crystal ball
(Jersey Museum)*

not be traced.

He was fined £2 a month with hard labour, and was bound over for a year and a day.

Even in the 1980s the credulity of the Islanders and the continuance of some superstitious practices persists. Nearly every parish, for example, has its 'charmer'. This is usually a woman who professes to cure, or charm away, what the medical profession have been unable to put right. There are also certain people on the Island who dabble in black magic. Some do so merely to bring extra excitement into their lives, others have the serious intention of trying to harm those who stand in their way or whom they dislike.

But black magic has a mysterious way of rebounding back on these dabblers. So, in the early 1980s, a clergyman was specially appointed by the Bishop of Winchester as his adviser on Exorcism for the whole of the Channel Isles. He deals with people seeking deliverance from evil forces which they feel are beyond their control. Without any publicity, he has been able – usually in the context of the Holy Communion Service – to bring peace to both places and people on the Island.

Tales from the Parishes

A General View

The final division of Jersey's forty-five square miles into twelve separate ecclesiastical entities, or parishes, was complete by about the year 1,000. Subsequently each parish was divided into vingtaines, with the exception of St Ouen, whose parochial subdivisions are called 'cueillettes'.

The parish is led in civil affairs by the Constable, whose honorary, elected position dates back as least as early as the fifteenth century. He heads the team of the parish's unpaid police force as well as representing the parish in the States Assembly. As he has no exact English equivalent – being an amalgam of Police Chief, Mayor and Member of Parliament – he is best described as being 'Father' of his parish.

The other members of the parish's honorary police force, who serve with the Constable, are the Procureurs (trustees), the Centeniers, the most senior of whom is known as 'Le Chef de Police'; as many Vingteniers as the parish has vingtaines, with one, two, or more Constable's Officers to each vingtaine. All the posts are elected and as there is a strong tradition of community service in Jersey, it is considered a great privilege to stand for one of these demanding and time-consuming honorary positions in one's own parish.

The parish church is no longer the important centre of parochial life that once it was. From the eleventh century – by which time most of the churches had been built – until the nineteenth century it used to be the place where all meetings were held and all official announcements made. It was also where any penance decided on by the Dean's Court for a parishioner's moral transgression – such as playing cards on a Sunday or adultery – was publicly carried out. For at least 200 years after the Reformation, so great was the desire of most parishioners to be included in all the activities of their parish church, that to be excommunicated – 'shut off as a septic limb from the fellowship of the Church' – was the ultimate deterrent.

But during the 900 years the parish church has been in constant use, depending on both the religion and architectural fashion of the time, there have been many alterations to its appearance. All of them, as we have seen, suffered the transformation from Catholic church to Calvinist temple, for example.

Then, before 1550, each church had had its own peal of bells. But, at about that time, King Edward VI appointed a Royal Commission to look into how many 'objects of superstition' in Jersey churches might be sold for the benefit of the royal coffers. So included in the list were 'all the Parish Church Bells, with the exception of one, [which] were taken down and sold for the use and benefit of the King'. Sir Hugh Paulett, the Governor of Jersey, was empowered to put this order into effect but, in fact, did not do so until about thirty years later.

Sir Henry Spelman gives a contemporary account of what happened to the bells: 'At the end of Queen Mary's days (Callis being taken), Sir Hugh Paulett pulled down the bells of the Churches in Jersey; and sending them to St Malo in Brittany; fourteen of them were drowned at the entrance to that harbour; whereupon it is a bye-word at this day in those parts, when any strong east wind is blowing there to say 'The Bells of Jersey Now Ring'.'

As L'Amy recounts, the ringing of these fourteen foundered bells below the sea has gathered a further superstition:

> From the latter half of the 16th Century onwards, a strange superstition seems to have existed among Jersey mariners, to wit: that the unfortunate sailor who heard the pealing of submarine bells between the port of St. Helier and Minquier Rocks would never see land. Whenever men were drowned in this sinister locality the old folk used to say, 'Ils ont oui les clliochs des egllises de pâraisse' ('They have heard the bells of the Parish Churches').

Leading from each of the parish churches to the sea was what was known as a 'perquage' – a safe sanctuary path. These were the Church's way in the Middle Ages of extending the sanctuary, that the Church itself had always traditionally afforded, to a way of escape. Thus it offered, to members of its congregation who had transgressed the civil laws, an alternative to the trial and subsequent harsh punishment they could expect if they were convicted. There were many who preferred to take the perquage to voluntary and permanent exile, than endure such medieval refinements as the thumbscrew and the rack.

As Charles II in 1663 gave Sir Edouard de Carteret all these four foot-wide sanctuary paths as a gift, they are not now as visible as once they were. For Sir Edouard and his descendants gradually sold them off, often to adjoining landowners. However, St Brelade's perquage, the shortest one, has recently been reopened.

When the island was divided into royal gifts of land for loyal subjects in Norman times, these gifts were called 'fiefs'. Usually, but not always, the owners – Seigneurs – built themselves manors on their fiefs. These manors took the name of the fief, whose boundaries sometimes coincided with those of a parish. Therefore, although in every parish there is at least one Manor, and often more, not every parish has a manor named after it. There is, for example a Trinity Manor, but although in St Saviour there were four manors, not one had the same name as the parish.

The manors of St Ouen, Rozel in St Martin, and Samares in St Clement had the dubious distinction of being allowed their own manorial gallows. This meant that the Seigneur not only had the right to hang any malefactor from his fief on his own gallows but also to pocket his goods and property as well. These rights were strenuously defended – even as late as 1695.

Some of the Seigneurs were also given royal permission to build colombiers, which were huge towers with nesting-places for pigeons a handy ingredient for pigeon-pie! A colombier may have been a medieval status symbol but it was just another cause for grievance for neighbouring farmers on whose crops the birds fed.

There were further unpleasantnesses – duties that had to be performed for one's Seigneur. Up until the eighteenth century

Les Colombiers

not only did his colombier have to be cleared out from time to time – a messy business – but there was his hay to cut, his wood to cart, and his wine to fetch, among innumerable other tasks. In medieval times, a vassal was also expected to defend his Seigneur with his life – even stand hostage for him.

The rank of Seigneur has today dwindled to being little more than an estate-owner. But the senior Seigneurs do still have their day – twice a year – when the Assise d'Heritage sits. This is a ceremonial occasion, with halberdiers lining the route from the Bailiff's door to the Court Room where the proceedings take place. In front of the Bailiff, the twelve Jurats, the Viscount and his law officers and the Lieutenant-Governor, together with all advocates, these selected Seigneurs formally swear allegiance to their Sovereign with the one word 'garde'. This signifies that they are present and agree to be included in any expression of loyalty that is made.

Any visitor to Jersey in July or September is likely to see an earnest group of men in each parish, solemnly measuring the height from the ground of any overhanging branch. The group will consist of the parish Constable, Centeniers, Vingteniers, Road Committee and road inspectors and they will be checking to see that no branch is nearer a footpath than eight feet and no nearer a road than twelve feet from the ground. This biannual inspection is called 'Visites du Branchage' and anyone found not to have lopped their branches to the correct height may be fined up to £50, or up to £2,000 if the case goes to court.

Each parish has its own distinctive badge, which will be described and explained in the appropriate section.

St Brelade

This parish has St Aubin's Fort to protect its eastern harbour and a lighthouse with the ill-omened name of La Corbière, the raven, to warn of its dangerous south-western tip. Summer visitors are particularly attracted by its wide bay – once the haunt of smugglers – and its Fishermen's Chapel, Among its famous sons was Jean Martel, the brandy merchant.

A question mark hangs over the origin of the parish's name – the church could either have been dedicated to St Brendan, the navigator saint, or to St Bren Gwaladr, a Celtic companion of St Sampson who visited Jersey in the sixth century. Whichever saint it was, his personal symbol – a silver fish on a blue ground – has become the emblem of the parish.

How many people today, looking at St Brelade's Church in its unusual sea setting, would guess that its foundations were first laid elsewhere? Its original site, so legend tells us, was three-quarters of a mile away, near a pagan shrine. The workmen had started on the foundations, piled all the stones and tools neatly ready for the next day but when they had arrived for work in the morning – nothing was there. Eventually they found everything, laid out just as they had left it – but nearly a mile away, right by the side of the sea.

Thinking the seashore an unsuitable place to build a church, especially as most of the inhabitants lived near their original site, the workmen carted all the stones and tools back and began all over again. But the next morning not a sign of their building remained – once again everything had been transported to the seashore site. The builders then thought they saw the hand of God in what had happened and decided that the Divine wish was for a church whose walls would be washed by the sea, so they continued the building where twice the materials had been left.

According to which legend you read, either the Devil had the last laugh, because this site was so far from the majority of the congregation; or the fairies were the ones best pleased – though exhausted with twice humping around all those heavy stones, at least they had got their pagan shrine back for themselves!

Change, not of plan but of terrain, is a feature of another part of the parish. Les Quennevais was so named because it was 'une chanevière' – a place where hemp is grown. When Jersey was famous for its shipbuilding, hemp was used to make the many ship's ropes – and so was an important crop, needing fertile soil.

Tradition has it that one night local wreckers with a series of false lights lured a fleet of Spanish ships, brimful of New World treasure, to their doom on the rocks. Just before the last of the ships sank, the leader of the Spanish expedition stood on its deck and cursed the wreckers, prophesying that before the end of the year a terrible punishment would be meted out to them.

Three hundred and sixty-four fearful days passed but, to the wreckers' relief, absolutely nothing had happened to them. So, on the very last day of the prophesied year, they decided to celebrate their escape from whatever fate had had in store for them. But, just as they were settling down to their feast, the most terrible storm arose and lashed the sea right over the land. Every wrecker was drowned and when the sea retreated it left the whole area covered with sand and, therefore, barren – as it remains to this day.

Another sad tale is connected with the small island in Portelet Bay. Many visitors have the tower on Ile au Guerdain pointed out to them and are told it marks the tomb of a sailor called Janvrin. The tower is, in fact, one built by the British Government against the French nearly a hundred years after Janvrin's death.

The true story is that St Brelade-born Philip Janvrin went to Nantes in his ship Esther but, in 1721, was not allowed to bring the ship back into port because of the plague then raging in that part of France. For fear of infection the ship and its crew had to remain in quarantine in Belcroute Bay. There poor Philip Janvrin died but still his body was not allowed ashore. Finally permission was given for him to be buried on the Ile au Guerdain, in sight of his St Brelade home. The stone his widow eventually erected over his grave was probably broken up when the Martello Tower was built there in 1811.

Perhaps the most famous lovers to stay in St Brelade were General Boulanger and his mistress Madame de Bonnemain. At the end of the 1880s the General, as the French Minister of War, had gained enormous popularity in France both with the army and with the civilian population. He had been elected a Parisian Deputy with a majority of over a quarter of a million votes and seemed ready to overthrow the French Government and become Europe's first dictator.

Then, just hours away from the planned coup, his mistress Madame de Bonnemain had some trumped up charge brought against her by his political opponents. Frightened that she would be arrested, Madame de Bonnemain fled to Brussels and the General, in his love for her, followed. The Boulanger movement disbanded almost immediately, for, as they complained: 'We thought he was Caesar: he turned out to be only Romeo.'

Eventually the lovers settled in St Brelade, choosing a villa – built by an eccentric Parisian collector called Vanier – since demolished by Hotel L'Horizon. There they lived for two years, still planning to overthrow the French Government – one day. Then Madame de Bonnemain fell ill and went to Brussels for special treatment. It was of no avail and there she died. Unable to live without her, General Boulanger also went to Brussels and there, by her grave-side, blew out his brains.

The parish has been marked by hate as well as love. When in the seventeenth century, thousands of French Protestants fled to Jersey for safety from religious persecution, there was a house in St Aubin where they seemed particularly welcomed. Its owner would wait on the quay for the boats crowded with refugees to arrive, then he would invite them to stay at his house. There they would be entertained most hospitably – until nightfall. Then the host would turn murderer and kill them for their money. The horrifying screams that came from the victims terrified the neighbourhood. But not just at the time of their murders. The screams continued long after the murderer himself was dead, until in the end the 'House of Death', as it was called – to put a final end to the death shrieks – had to be pulled down.

About twelve years ago on Mont Nicolle, a man who regularly passed that way had a peculiar sensation every time he passed a certain garden that had in it a small random-built granite hut. Later it happened that he had the chance to meet the owner of the property and tell him about its unpleasant aura. The owner offered to take him into the hut which was about sixteen feet long and eight feet wide with a small window, and housing garden tools and such like.

The man decided that he would prefer to go into the hut alone, so he did – and explained later that it was like 'closing the lid on a coffin'. He came out almost immediately with the worst headache he had ever experienced in his life. Later he learned that in that hut, in the last part of the 1800s, a man had hanged himself.

St Clement

No wonder that this smallest of Jersey's parishes has St Clement as its patron. For the story is that this third Pope after St Peter was martyred by being lashed to an anchor and thrown into the Crimean Sea. He has always, therefore, had special care of sailors, and the sailors round the coastline of this parish, as well as the inhabitants of the often-flooded land, certainly need his protection. This is how Sir Gilbert Parker in his *Battle of the Strong* describes what he calls this 'terrible coast':

> You may range the seas, and you will find no such landing-place for imps of men as the field of rocks on the south-east corner of Jersey, called, with a malicious irony, the Banc des Violettes. The great rocks rise up like volcanic monuments from a floor of lava and trailing vraic, which at half-tide makes the sea a tender mauve and violet. The passages of safety between reefs are but narrow at high tide, and at half-tide, when the

currents are changing most, the violet-field becomes the floor of a vast mortuary chapel for unknowing mariners.

The parish also has many remnants of both pagan and superstitious beliefs. There are three from prehistory: Mont Ubé with its twenty eight upright stones marking a passage grave; La Motte – Green Island – where human remains have been discovered in some of the eighteen cist graves on the islet; and, sited half-way between the two, an object of stone worship for many centuries, the eleven-foot-high menhir known as 'La Dame Blanche'. The forty-foot-high granite rock known as 'Rocqueberg', was – as we have read – the supposed centre of the sixteenth-seventeenth-century witch movement.

From medieval times, in the south transept of the parish church are the remains of a fifteenth-century wall-painting that illustrated a popular poem of the time, 'The Three Living and the Three Dead'. It tells of three hunters met by three skeletons, who warn them of the vanity of all worldly pleasures. All that is left of this pictorial moral tale are two hunting dogs and the legs of two of the horses with the verse in French underneath, 'Alas, St Mary, who are these three corpses who look so grim? It breaks my heart to see them so piteous.'

The chief dwelling in the parish is Samares Manor, which takes its name from a corruption of the Old French 'salse Marais' – salt water marsh. Certainly the Seigneurs of Samares used to find the salt deposits, left by the ebbing tide on the flat marshy ground between the manor and the sea, an important source of income.

And what a proud family they were, too! When Peter de Sausmarez was summoned to the court of Common Pleas in 1300 to explain why he behaved in his extensive fief as if he were king, he was pat with his reply. He defended his right to keep a pair of gallows, have a warren, claim shipwrecks, to chase after rabbits over where Fort Regent now stands and to keep hawks – all considered royal privileges in those days – with these proud words: 'That he and his ancestors were in possession from time immemorial of the said Manor and had free liberty to chase over all the Mount of St Helier with their hunting dogs, ferrets, nets and hunting poles.' To which defence the Court of Pleas had no reply!

To the seigneural perk of being shipped by his tenants, at least once in their lives, to any one of the four Norman ports whenever he wanted a free trip to France, was added a special bonus for his Dame. If she happened to be living in the Fief du Hommet, a subsidiary of the Samares fief, when she had a baby, then it was the Rector of St Clement's job to provide her with a white horse on which to ride to church for her Churching service.

The inhabitants of St Clement were open to superstitious suggestion long after the last witch from their parish was tried and sentenced to death. The focal point of their imagination was a blood curdling roar which was heard in the vicinity of La Grande Charrière every time there was an exceptionally low tide. In no time at all, it was decided that there was a great bull, big as a house and with eyes of fire, who roamed about the reefs of 'Les Grands Hommets' at low tide. So strong was the belief that even some of the fishermen confessed that they were frightened to go fishing after its roar had been heard.

Then one of a sand-eeling party on Les Grands Hommets decided to seek a rational explanation for the roaring of the Bull of St Clement. This he did, nearly frightening the life out of his companions as he tested his theory. He had found a formation in the rocks below a pool which acted like a waste pipe when the water from the pool poured down it at low tide. The gurgling as it went down reverberated in that rocky environment to such an extent that on a calm day its echo could be heard the whole length of the St Clement coastline. The sand-eeling party decided – for the good of the St Clementais' nerves – to plug the hole, and so died the Bull of St Clement!

A famous visitor to St Clement who was not averse to dabbling in the supernatural was the exile Victor Hugo. During the three years that he and his family lived at No. 3 Marine Terrace, Grève D'Azette, he used to spend many of his days behind closed shutters – so as not to shock the natives. What was he up to? One of his guests was a certain Madame Girardin who brought with her the latest Paris craze – table turning. On the evening of 6 September 1853, under her instruction, the whole Hugo family gathered round

Victor Hugo

the table. Nothing happened. Undismayed, Madame Girardin put the lack of response down to the fact that the table was square!

A round table was then bought, and began to speak; the first Sunday it was tried out they were in communication with a young girl who had recently died. Once Madame Girardin had left, Victor Hugo put himself in charge of the table-turning and his contacts were far more spectacular than an unknown dead girl. Reports of the seances were taken down as they took place and later published in book form – but not until after his death, at his own request. 'This book,' he said of it, 'will certainly be one of the bibles of the future.'

His contacts were with men of the same genius as himself. There was Shakespeare, who naturally spoke in verse, then Luther, with whom Hugo held long theological discussions, and supreme contact of all – Jesus Christ himself. He was reported to have replied on 11 February 1855, at half past nine in the evening. They had several religious conversations together and, on 22 March, Christ defined his principles and his religion as 'a door of light with a night lock'. With such guests from the other world, no wonder Victor Hugo and his family spent whole days round the table!

Victor Hugo also took much delight in all Jersey's monstrously shaped rocks and caves. So, despite photography being still in its infancy, he had Gothic shots taken of himself, posing poetically in their vicinity.

A more recent contact with the supernatural took place on a staircase. In a house in St Clement workmen had been asked to demolish the old staircase to make way for a modern one. Once they had begun their work, the ghost of a woman, dressed in a long grey garment, was seen on the stairway. A local clairvoyant was called in, because it was known that a woman had once fallen down those stairs and died as the result of the accident. When the clairvoyant saw the lady in grey, she explained to her that the staircase had to be removed, and then told the family that when she herself went out of their house the grey lady would go too. She did.

Grouville

As the old form of this parish's name was 'Grosville', and 'villa' betokened a farm with a great deal of land attached to it, it suggests that the area was dominated by someone with a particularly large estate. The church, therefore, did not bear the same name as the parish – but was dedicated to St Martin.

This chief tomato-growing parish has two notable landmarks within its boundaries. The first is the prehistoric dolmen at Hougue Bie with the chapel dedicated to Our Lady of the Dawn on its summit. The second is the oldest windmill in the Island which, without its sails, has been preserved by the British Admiralty as a landmark to guide ships safely to harbour on that reef-strewn coast.

Grouville Common has always been a favourite spot to visit, though not always to enjoy the majestic sweep of the Bay, which so impressed Queen Victoria that it was allowed to add the epithet 'Royal' to its name. In those hot-tempered days, when honour had to be satisfied, it was a favourite spot for duellers. Then, in 1843, the horse-racing which had previously taken place on St Aubin's sand and later at Grève D'Azette was transferred to

Grouville's 160 vergées of dry sandy heath, bordering the sea. For the next six years, as the painting by Ouless depicts, the races became the focal point of the Island's magnificent annual carnival.

Jersey Races, Grouville Common 1949, by P.J. Ouless (Barreau Art Gallery, Jersey Museum)

Grouville's former Constable, Alan Le Maistre, can trace the site of his Manor farm back to 1170. Originally known as La Maletière, it belonged to Robert Malet when he was Seigneur of the Fie. One of its oldest parts is a tourelle or spiral stone staircase – possibly the best example in Jersey. Most unusually for such an historic building, since the twelfth century it has only been sold twice – the second time in 1841 to the Constable's great-great-grandfather, Pierre Le Maistre.

Incredibly, Grouville Parish extends fifteen miles to the south of Jersey to include the Minquiers – a group of tiny islands known locally as the 'Minkeys'. Traditionally, parishioners have had the prerogative to fish there and sleep there but, starting in the nineteenth century, the French became increasingly interested in claiming sovereignty over the archipelago for the sake of its growing fishy harvest. They began to interfere with Islanders' fishing-nets and removed their lobster-pots.

In 1952 the whole matter was referred to the International Court of Justice at The Hague. A year later the Court decided in favour of Britain and, therefore, Jersey. Now the Jersey authorities pay regular visits and the Union Jack is periodically hoisted on Flagstaff Hill, at the northern end of the Maîtresse Ile.

No. 1 Tower (Grouville Bay), La Rocque, by Alexander Shepherd (Jersey Museum)

St Helier

The Parish of St Helier takes its name from the Saint who lived for fifteen years as a hermit on a rock in St Aubin's Bay – and its emblem with the two axes from the manner of his death.

Born at Tongres in Belgium, Helier, who began his life as Helibert, has many legends told about him. To begin with, his pagan parents had quite despaired of having any children and so when a Christian missionary, Cunibert, moved into their area, they hurried to consult him. He told them that they would have a son if they promised to allow the child to become a Christian and be brought up by himself. Of course, they promised this.

But once a son had been born to them, it seemed hard to part with him and year after year they delayed sending him to Cunibert. Then suddenly, in his seventh year, Helibert, who had been so healthy up to that time, developed paralysis of the legs. His parents hesitated no longer and sent the crippled boy to Cunibert forthwith.

Once with the missionary, Helibert's paralysis was immediately cured, so he was given the name Helier, which means pity, because God had taken pity on him and cured him. Then Cunibert instructed the young boy in the Christian faith and enlisted his help in the garden.

There Helier had an immediate problem – rabbits. Not one of his vegetables was left unnibbled. So he came to an agreement with them – he would draw a line down his garden and the rabbits could eat all they wanted down one side, if they promised to leave what he grew on the other side severely alone. And it worked!

One day, however, a crafty hunter thought to catch some of the rabbits as they feasted on their side of the line, but as his horse leapt over the demarcation, he was hit in the eye by an overhanging bough and blinded. Helier, when he saw him in his plight, made the Sign of the Cross over him and he was able to see again.

All this time Helier's parents were rather envious of all the attention their son was paying to Cunibert and the work he was doing in the Christian's garden, so they tried to entice him home, but Helier remembered the promise they had given and so refused to come. Then Helier's father took matters in his own hands – he had Cunibert assassinated.

The young Helier was horrified at what had happened and ran away. Eventually, after several years in penitential retreat in a disused chapel, Helier sought out the Christian Marcouf at Nanteuil for guidance as to what he should do with his life. Marcouf first baptised Helier and then suggested that he come to Jersey with the more experienced Christian, Romard, as his companion.

Helier chose for his dwelling a high rock at the far end of a small island reached from the south coast of Jersey at low tide by a causeway about half a mile long. Here he built himself a primitive cell, the remains of which are known to this day as the Hermitage. From that vantage point, Helier was able by his miraculous power to keep the marauding Normans away from the terrified Islanders, until one day – fifteen years after his arrival – when the pirates returned to have their revenge. Seeing them coming, Romard hurried to get help from the Islanders at the other end of the causeway. He left Helier praying. The Normans found him alone on the seashore and with their axes cut off his head.

Marcouf founded a monastery near the Hermitage in memory of the martyr, which remained an important force for the religious and secular instruction of the Islanders for 400 years. By the time of the Reformation, though, the building had fallen into ruins except for its church and the Order had dwindled to a handful of monks. Then, in the last decade of the sixteenth century, the islet became part of the defence of Jersey against invaders and in 1603 the newly built fortifications were officially named Elizabeth Castle.

The Governor's residence was then moved from Mont Orgueil to Elizabeth Castle. From 1600 to 1603 Sir Walter Raleigh was Jersey's Governor, although the active time he spent in the Island during that period was only a matter of a few months. More importantly, it was in Elizabeth Castle that King Charles II gave the name of New Jersey to an island off the coast of Virginia – the first of Jersey's attempts to colonise the New World!

Many stories are told about Charles's exile in Jersey when, after the news came through of his father's execution, he had been proclaimed King here in 1649. Nothing shows more of his easy-going nature than this tale told of his French friend – a dwarfish Doctor of Divinity. Too much learning had affected the mind of this dwarf and so Charles kept him on at Court as an unofficial jester. One Sunday, it came into the dwarf's head to imagine himself a monkey and give a monkey's sermon from the town church pulpit in front of the King.

So, much to the congregation's surprise, there, just over the top of the pulpit, appeared this ugly little face. The Lieutenant-Governor, George de Carteret, rushed to the pulpit, got hold of the dwarf and hustled him out of the church. The service continued, but after a few minutes, three great stones came crashing through the church window, one narrowly missing the King's head. Was the dwarf punished? Not at all – he was just presented with a new suit of clothes and a purseful of money and sent back to France.

Two early chapels built in St Helier after the town's conversion to Christianity were the Chapelle de la Madelaine, near the site of the present parish church, and Notre Dame des Pas on the eastern slope of Town Hill. The first owed its name to its dedication to St Mary Magdalene, but there are conflicting theories to explain the name of the second. Some authorities point to the fact that long before Notre Dame des Pas was built, there was a ring of thirty upright stones marking a prehistoric burial-place on the summit

of Town Hill where Fort Regent now is. This was known as 'La Pouquelaye des Pas' – a fairy place. Therefore, this theory has Notre Dame to refer not to Our Lady, the Virgin Mary, but to the fairy who inhabited the Pouquelaye.

The second explanation concerns what seem to be two footprints that were on a rock just off Green Street. The Virgin Mary is supposed to have appeared just at this spot and, where she stood, left the imprint of her feet. So the Chapel was dedicated to Our Lady of the Footprints. Or could Pas just be a misprint for Pace – meaning Peace? For just to the east of La Collette is a little haven where ships could find safe anchorage from the storms that so often lash that coast.

As the town of St Helier grew and became the administrative centre of the Island, places had to be found where those who transgressed the States Acts could be punished in full view of as many Islanders as possible as a horrible deterrent. So, as we have seen, the stocks were in the parish churchyard; floggings and executions often took place in the market-place where the Royal Square now is. But there was also, after the sixteenth century, a gallows erected on the 250-foot-high hill west of the town. From the four gaunt pillars of execution on its summit, it was called Le Mont ès Pendus or Le Mont Patibulaire – the Mount of Hanging. Until comparatively recently it was also known as Gallows Hill, but the new name of Westmount now hides its former grisly associations.

The man who carried out the frequent executions – hanging was the punishment for stealing anything worth more than a shilling was known as the Maître des Hautes OEuvres, the Master of High Deeds. His salary was twenty-five crowns a year, a tied cottage at Bel Royal, plus the clothes of the criminal. These were often bought back by the bereaved family at exorbitant prices, so that the body would not be left to hang naked on the gibbet.

Before an execution, a notice of its taking place next market day would be read out in church and schoolmasters were told to close their schools, so that their pupils could witness exactly what breaking the law led to. The prisoner himself would be led by hallebardiers to walk from the prison up the hill, unless his crime were particularly heinous. If this were so, he was dragged to the hill's summit on a hurdle, to show those watching that he was too evil to be allowed to touch the ground lest he pollute it.

> *I vaut mûs alouonyi l'bras qu'le co.*
> *Better stretch the arm than the neck, or –*
> *Laziness leads to the gallows.*

There are three recorded cases which show what brutal events these executions were. In 1640, when the criminal already had the rope round his neck, he suddenly threw the hangman off the scaffold, swarmed up one of the pillars and defied anyone to bring him down. No one did, until the Vicomte took the scaffold ladder and with it prodded him off his perch. As he fell, the halter round his neck tightened and so he did not escape his hanging after all. But was the Vicomte guilty of murder? Only the official executioner was authorised to take a life on such occasions.

Nearly 200 years later, in 1807, a soldier was sentenced to be hanged for the murder of a watchmaker. Once hanging from the gibbet, he seemed to take such a long time to die that the hangman, to bring the matter to a swift conclusion, hung on to the soldier's legs. But instead of this tightening the halter round the murderer's neck, the hangman's added weight only stretched the rope. This allowed the soldier's feet to touch the ground whereupon he immediately took the rope off from round his neck. As no man can be hanged twice, he eventually gained the King's Pardon.

The third case concerned the last execution ever to be held on Gallows Hill. In 1829 Philippe Join was being executed, in front of a large crowd, for the murder of his father. First he made a speech from the scaffold, attributing his downfall to drink and acknowledging the righteousness of his punishment. Then a white bag was pulled over his head; the Burial Service was read to him; and finally, the trapdoor on which he stood was opened, so that the rope about his neck would tighten and he would be hanged. A comment on the execution in the local paper read, 'Let us hope that the execution of this terrible sentence has touched the hearts of parents, and taught them a stern lesson that will lead them to control their children's actions with stricter vigilance. Pray God above all that the young people present may profit by it.'

It was just as well for Marie Le Gendre that by 1846 public executions were a thing of the past, for after her crime not only did she live to tell the sad tale but also to marry again. She and her husband apparently kept a house of ill-repute at Mulberry Cottage in Patriotic Street. When the Centenier George Le Cronier, accompanied by the Constable's Officer, arrived there to arrest the pair, only Mrs Le Gendre was at home. When the Centenier attempted to arrest her, she got hold of a carving-knife and drove it straight into his stomach. 'O, mon garçon, je suis stabbé,' groaned the Centenier.

The Constable's Officer deftly avoided a second lunge of the carving-knife and dashed out of the house, crying 'Murder! Murder!' Poor George Le Cronier died the next day – the only Centenier in Jersey to be killed in the course of duty. Marie Le Gendre was tried for his murder and banished. Later it was heard that she had married again, and, by an ironic coincidence, her new name was - Mrs Le Cronier! The twenty-five-foot-high granite memorial to the Centenier erected by his parish is at the southern end of Green Street Cemetery.

It would be strange, indeed, if a town as old as St Helier did not have visitations from the past and the following stories show that these still occur:

Cronier Monument, St Helier

In Old St John's Road there is a house that had the reputation of being haunted. In the 1930s and 1940s so eerie were the sounds and smells that came from it that nobody would live in it. Then came the German Occupation and the house was commandeered for army personnel. But even the Germans stayed only a matter of months. The house then remained empty right up until the early 1950s. After that it appears there was no more trouble, as it has been continuously occupied ever since.

In the early 1970s in St James's Street there was the story of the mother and her teenage daughter being terrorised by a male ghost. The young girl was the one who seemed to suffer most. In her presence clocks came off the wall, objects were thrown across the room. When she was in bed she often felt a cold presence in the room and a breathless sensation, as if the ghost were trying to stifle her.

As the girl's father had recently died and had left no indication where he had hidden some missing money, she and her mother thought that the ghost might be her father's spirit come back to tell them where it was. It transpired afterwards that the house had been built over an old graveyard and that until the house had been exorcised neither the mother nor her daughter would have any peace.

The next two incidents occurred between fifteen and twenty years ago when each policeman had his own beat which he patrolled on foot. A policeman had just finished his spell of duty in Conway Street at about one o'clock in the morning when he saw a man approaching from New Cut. He had a raincoat on and there was something peculiar about his appearance. So while his colleague went into a pub for something to eat, he followed the man to check what he was up to. The man turned into Bond Street and then completely disappeared. The policeman searched all the side alleys but could find no trace of the man. On rejoining his colleague he described his fruitless search. But his colleague looked at him in astonishment. 'What man?' he asked. 'I didn't see anyone.'

One night very late this same policeman was walking on the south side of Broad Street just past the Electricity Company. Then he noticed that a soldier was standing in the road outside the Jersey Dairies. He was wearing No. 1 Blues with a high collar but he wore no hat. As the policeman watched him, he walked into a side door where no one lived and just disappeared into the building.

A teenage lad living in Winchester Street was always very

impatient with an elderly spinster schoolteacher who lodged with the family in their front room. He was very pleased, therefore, when the time came for him to leave home and join the Forces.

When he came home on leave from his Parachute Regiment and went to bed in his own room for the first time after his long absence, he noticed that the moon was shining so brightly it would have been possible to read the newspaper headlines by it. Then as he was dozing he had a peculiar feeling. So he opened his eyes. There, bending over him was the elderly lodger from the front room. She was outlined by the brilliant moon to such an extent, that he could see the strands of her untidy grey hair and the fluff from her mohair shawl. He was absolutely stricken with fear and remorse – the elderly schoolteacher had been dead for over four years.

St Helier has also seen the practice of black magic. Not so long ago there was a witch supposed to be living near West Park. But, when the cow that a saddler owned fell sick and he was convinced that it had been bewitched, he was not quite sure who to blame. Whether he boiled pins, which would cause the guilty person such discomfort that she would come and confess, or whether he used some other method is not known. All he would say was, 'We found the bugger.' It was the lady at West Park – and the cow recovered.

More recently, in 1981, a man moved his already established health food shop to new premises in Beresford Street. Part of his plan was to knock the small rooms on the first floor into one large one to serve as a restaurant. In carrying out this renovation, the workmen had to take up the lino. As they did so, they discovered some marks painted on the floorboards, some literature referring to black magic and a silver coin placed under the boards.

The man immediately got in touch with a local clairvoyant who, on seeing the boards, said that there was no doubt that they were part of a black magic ritual. In the centre of a square was an anvil and the points of the compass. The outline of the square itself included tulips in its pattern, which have specific sexual connotations. There was an entrance to the square but no exit. Her advice to him was to burn the boards immediately and be in no way tempted to use them. She also suggested that he might be wiser to leave the premises altogether.

The man, being sceptical about supernatural interference, did not take the advice given him. He stayed on and was quite pleased that the publicity given to his new enterprise by the finding of the boards gave it such a profitable send-off. But almost immediately, despite eventually presenting the boards to the Museum, it seemed that things began to go wrong. His misfortunes increased to such an extent that eighteen months after the finding of the black magic boards, he decided to sell his share in the business and quit the Beresford Street premises.

Although the boards were thought to have been painted as recently as the German Occupation, yet the house itself has a history of strange happenings. For a long time it was quite common to see a hideous old woman sitting in an oak chair at the top of the stairs – but there was no old woman living in the house at the time.

To those who live in the country parishes, inhabitants of St Helier have always seemed different – less 'vrais Jersiaises' somehow! Country people used to call the yobbos who skulked about St Helier's streets up to no good, 'town pats'. For townees in general, they had the splendidly dismissive label 'les clyichards' – those suffering from diarrhoea!

> *Pot d'pichi n'est pas profit*
> *Sus la tête d'un offici.*
> *It does not pay to assault the police, literally*
> *'to break a pot on the head of an officer.'*

St John

In the Middle Ages the largest fair of the whole Island used to be held in this parish. On Midsummer's Day, also the festival of the parish's patron saint – St John the Baptist, people from every corner of the Island used to congregate at Bonne Nuit Bay. Once there, the idea was to get themselves rowed once round the rock, Le Cheval Guillaume, in order to avoid bad luck for the rest of the year.

By the time the lively Philippe Dumaresq, founder of one of Jersey's first newspapers, came to live in the parish in 1792, the whole celebration had become rather tame. As he explained in his *Gazette*: 'For years an old custom has drawn on St John's Day a very large concourse of people to enjoy the insipid amusement of being rowed in a boat round a rock. That done, there was nothing to do but to drink gin and cider.'

So to liven the patronal festival up a bit, Philippe Dumaresq introduced a two-day fair on the lines of the fairs held in France. He erected no fewer than fifty tents to sell everything from lace to butter; there was an open-air market for livestock; and for entertainment there were tight-rope-walkers and comedy turns. A whole ox was roasted and the fair ended with a massive firework display.

He was, alas, too successful in his attempts to bring a little life to the parish. After five years the fair was closed down for good, because the States decreed it was 'contrary to good morals'! But the traditions associated with the day before, St John's Eve, continued and are vividly described by two early-nineteenth-century writers. In 1809 Stead wrote:

In the Parish [St John's], and indeed in most parts of the Island, a custom prevails of which the Origin is unknown; on the Eve of St. John's Day, several Persons in different Parts of the several Parishes assemble their respective Neighbours, a large Brass Boiler, (in ordinary uses as a Kitchen Utensil), is taken into the Yard and partly filled with Water, in which spoons, drinking Utensils, Candlesticks, etc. of Metal, are immersed; a strong species of Rush is tied; having been thoroughly wetted, Persons of both Sexes then lay hold of each Rush, and drawing their Hands quickly upwards and often repeating the Application, cause a Vibration of the Boiler and other Articles that produces a most dolorous and terrific Sound, which is increased by the blowing of Cow's Horns: the Exercise forms altogether a discordant Noise, almost as loud as a Chinese Gong. This uncommon Amusement is continued for several Hours, 'till the Performers are weary and deafened with their Sport. It is called, faire braire les Poeles; the same Custom prevails in the neighbouring Province of Normandy.

William Plees, writing eight years later, went on to describe how out of hand affairs became once the 'faire braire les Poeles' was over:

How extraordinary soever this recreation may be, it would be well if it ended in the innocent though discordant manner just described but, unhappily, it has introduced another custom, which is of an injurious nature. After the sport is over, parties of men and boys go about the country, and from all the cows they can find take the milk, for sillibubs, puddings, etc. for the following day. They also make depredations in the gardens. This conclusive amusement is however now much restrained, and by magisterial vigilance will, probably, in a few years be entirely suppressed.

Is Cheval Rock, as the lucky rock in Bonne Nuit Bay is now called, really a rock? According to legend – definitely not. For in the waters round the Bay lived a mischievous and rather tiresome kelpie whose idea of a joke was to stir up the sea to boiling pitch and then watch the boats unable to ride the waves disappear under them.

These cruel ways had endeared him to none of his own kind, so he decided that if he was ever to find a wife she would have to be human. As his magic only had power in the sea and at night, the sole chance he would ever have of picking a bride would be at full moon, when the young girls from St John came down to Bonne

Nuit Bay to see how long it would be before they were married. If the stone they skimmed across the sea in the moonlight made one ripple, they were much happier than if it made several – for each ripple signified a month's long wait before the husband-to-be would turn up to claim his bride.

On this particular evening of the full moon, the girls came giggling down to the beach, and as they stooped to pick their stone, he immediately chose the most beautiful of them all – Anne-Marie – as his future bride. Instantly he put his magic power into effect, and as Anne-Marie skimmed her stone across the moonlit water, thinking of her soldier lover William away at the war, it sank straight to the bottom – it had not made even one ripple.

Then to her surprise, right at the water's edge appeared a figure she recognised – William. He must have been granted leave and, hearing where she had gone with the other girls, had stolen to the beach to surprise her. She rushed across the sand and threw herself into his arms. But the arms that clasped her tight in return were damp and clammy, the tenacious grip that held her was dragging her under the waves.

By an incredible stroke of good fortune, just before the kelpie could manage to drag Anne-Marie to the marriage-bed of seaweed he had prepared for her on the floor of the sea, the first cock to announce daybreak began to crow. Immediately the kelpie felt his

magic power go from him; he was unable to hold on to Anne-Marie any longer. He disappeared under the waves raging with disappointment: Anne Marie was washed up on the beach unconscious.

The poor girl told no one what had happened that moonlit night, only made quite sure that she stayed as far away from the sea as possible. That is until her lover William came home from the wars and suggested that they should take a walk along the shore, something he had been longing to do all the time he had been away fighting. Not even Anne-Marie's tears, nor her tale of being dragged into the sea by a kelpie made any difference. 'No kelpie would ever dare to come near you, with me and my trusty sword by your side', he boasted, and he dragged her right to the water's edge.

There, as they walked, he told her all about his exploits abroad, the death in battle of his noble horse and his hope, for the sake of the honour it would bring, to go to war again as soon as he could find a suitable charger. Anne-Marie listened to his plans for the future with dread in her heart. What if the kelpie came for her again while William was away?

On the day before his planned sailing from Bonne Nuit, he went to his now disused stable, to get the bridle and saddle ready for the charger he would buy as soon as he could find one. But the stable was not empty – there, where his old horse used to stand, was a powerful, pure-white stallion. William could not believe his eyes. Who could have presented him with such a perfect gift? William had never seen the horse to equal it in all his life. Now there would be no question of what a fine figure he would cut on the field of battle.

That night William went to bed full of high hopes, thinking that even Anne-Marie would be won over to his plans once she saw the splendid white horse. But William's sleeping thoughts were not so pleasant. A figure came to warn him in his dream against an unknown foe. This foe was so cunning that only the charm of mistletoe could prevail against his wily tricks.

The dream seemed so real that despite there being such little time before his boat left, William got up before it was light and walked all the way to Rozel where he knew he could be sure of finding a piece of mistletoe. He pushed a sprig of it into his doublet, and got home just in time to saddle his white charger, take a fond farewell of Anne Marie and meet the other soldiers ready to embark.

Just as William was cantering towards the group of armed men on the beach, his white horse swerved and started a headlong gallop into the sea. Desperately he pulled on the reins, shouted at the horse to stop – but to no avail. The horse was already up to his neck in water, its beautiful white mane floating on the sea. Then it was that William begun to realise that the horse he was riding was no ordinary beast. Was it one of the cunning and deadly tricks that the figure in his dream had warned him of?

William plucked the mistletoe from his doublet and brought it down sharply on the horse's head. The stallion gave a horrifying yell, instantly stopped his plunge under the waves and began to stiffen. It gave one last tremor of life and turned into rock.

What became of William, whether Anne-Marie ever married, her headstrong soldier, and what happened to the kelpie is not known. But the petrified white horse, William's horse, Le Cheval Guillaume, is still there in Bonne Nuit Bay for everyone to see and wonder at.

With witches and their cats meeting at Becquet ès Chats for their Sabbats and parishioners being struck blind if they happen to catch sight of the fairies at their ablutions just below Sorel at

Le Lavoir des Dames, it is not surprising to learn that there is at least one haunted house in the parish. No one has actually seen a ghost there – only heard strange noises.

An old gardener who was employed there at the end of the last century explained that there were two rooms in the house which were never used. This was because however securely the communicating door between them was locked, it was always found wide open the next day.

Then one night, while the old gardener was smoking his pipe by the kitchen fire with the door and windows closed, a sudden draught roared up the chimney. The noise it made seemed to the old man like the sound of souls in torment and he was just about to rush from the room in terror, when the noise stopped as abruptly as it began.

At another time he heard a knock on the door. When he went to open it, there was no one there. So he left the door open and went back into the room. But the tap, tap, tapping came again – this time on the vacant window-pane.

The parish was also known for two rather unusual ecclesiastical activities and one graveyard story. Before education in the Island was compulsory, the Rector was teacher as well as Pastor. And where did he teach his young charges? In the belfry! An inspection of the church tower revealed that once there had been two floor levels there – but still an odd place in which to find a school.

Then there were the angry Anti-pillarites. They were members of the congregation who objected to having their view of the pulpit blocked by a pillar if they sat in the south aisle. In 1828 the Rector was told by them to ask permission from the Ecclesiastical Court for its removal. He did not want to ask, because he thought that without the pillar his whole church would collapse. In 1831 the appeal was eventually made but the Court turned it down.

With the coming of a new Rector, the Anti-pillarites tried again and, as before, met with no success. But as Jerseymen seldom take 'no' for an answer, they just bided their time. Then the Rector left Jersey for a holiday in France. When he got back, he found the offending pillar in his garden, where it has stayed to this day.

The graveyard was not the Anglican one by the church but

Macpela in the south of the parish. It was so called after the burial place bought by Abraham for his wife Sarah and it was used by non-Anglicans who, by law, could not be buried in any of the parish churches. Its greatest fame came in the mid 1880s, when Jersey was full of refugees from Revolutions that were erupting all over Europe at that time.

Whenever one of these Revolutionaries died in exile in Jersey, all the rest would band together and march to his burial in Macpela behind the red flag. While Victor Hugo was also exiled here between 1852 and 1855, it was considered an honour for the great French poet to give the funeral oration. He used every one as an excuse to vilify his arch-enemy Napoleon III – the man who had ordered his expulsion from France.

It would be nice to conclude the tales from this Parish with a thrilling account of why the Wolf Caves on its northern coastline are so called. The truth is not so spectacular. That coastal strip was famous for its sea perch, and the French for sea perch is *loup de mer*. This, it is thought, when incorrectly translated, gave the caves their unusual name.

St Lawrence

This parish, Jersey's most central, has for its emblem the grid on which St Lawrence was roasted alive. The church dedicated to him was the last in the Island to be restored from its transformation as a Huguenot temple. Only in 1892 were its three-decker pulpit, high-backed pews, and special boxes for the gentry cleared away to be replaced by the present interior arrangements.

In its churchyard is a Latin epitaph for two of the Hamptonne family – an important one in the parish – which reads:

All is dust! [This is in Greek: the rest is Latin.] Hail, passer by!

I would have a word for thee for a moment. Within this Temple lies buried that illustrious man, Laurens Hamptonne, who deserved more than well of his country, once Vicomte of this island, and Lieutenant-Bailiff, and Captain of this Parish, now, alas, snatched from us. Born, 1600. Unborn 2 Feb., and buried 5 Feb 1664. Also Edouard Hamptonne, Junior. If anyone in this island was polished, it was he. He too was Vicomte, and now, alas, has been torn from us by an untimely death. Ripe for Heaven, he was taken away, 27 Jan. and buried on the 29th, 1660. Born, 1628. Farewell, passer by. Live in the light. Remember Death and Heaven.

The most hated place in the parish was the 'Hangman's Cottage', a tied cottage for the public executioner which was situated between Mainland and Bel Royal. The most feared place was Waterworks Valley, because of the ghostly procession that was supposed to haunt it.

The story goes that many years ago a young girl, all arrayed in her bridal finery, came down Waterworks Valley in her coach and six to be married in St Lawrence's Church. But the bridegroom never arrived. So the young girl had herself driven home again and once there committed suicide. Once a year, at midnight, she still rides down to church to the sound of church bells. Her coachman has white ribbons on his whip and the girl herself is dressed in all her bridal finery. Only as she passes will the terrified watcher see that she has no face – the white veil is draped round a grinning skull.

A more up-to-date horror is the building of the German Underground Hospital in the parish during the Occupation. The labour force used for its excavation were prisoners of war, who had been marched across Europe from the Ukraine, guarded by S.S. men and large savage dogs. In building the 200-yard-long parallel tunnels and six shorter connecting ones, 14,000 tons of rock had to be removed. Many of the slave workers were killed by the ensuing falls of stones and rock. They had no proper burial but are said to have been thrown behind the walls of the hospital before they were concreted over. So the thousands of tourists who visit this Occupation relic each year are, unknowingly, standing in a twentieth-century burial-chamber.

St Martin

St Martin of Tours is the patron saint of both Grouville and this parish's church, but this is the older dedication of the two. Inside the church is the ancient statue of the Saint, dividing his cloak in two to share it with a cold and starving beggar.

It was always thought of as the leading church in the island, especially since it provided so many deans, including Dean Mabon who built his Holy Sepulchre Chapel on the summit of Hougue Bie. But it had its moment of doubt and panic in 1616, when, one Sunday morning, its spire was struck by lightning and broke in the middle. It seemed to the Islanders a warning from God that something dire was about to befall Jersey. Had it not been written that, 'Judgement must begin at the House of God'?

The perquage – sanctuary path – went from the church and followed a stream until it came out near St Catherine's Tower. It was last used by Thomas Le Seeleur in 1646. He escaped death from hanging by just walking down the path and stepping into a boat that took him to Normandy.

Another criminal who – in the end – did not get off so lightly was Geoffroy. He had been convicted of a capital crime and his punishment was to be thrown off a high rock between Gorey and Anne Port and into the sea below. Many Islanders came to see justice done and watched Geoffroy being escorted to the headland by two halberdiers.

Then a masked executioner took hold of the prisoner and threw him down into the sea. To the amazement of the crowds, despite the huge drop, Geoffroy was seen to be swimming back to the shore. At this, some of the ladies present shouted that the prisoner should be thrown again, as the executioner obviously had not done his job thoroughly. Others shouted back that the sentence had been carried out, justice had been done and that the prisoner should now be allowed to go free.

It was Geoffroy himself who settled the argument. He offered to throw himself off the cliff to show how easily it could be done. This time, fatally for Geoffroy, his head struck a rock on his drop down, and he fell dead into the sea below.

The manor which has always dominated the parish is Rosel. It gets its name from its first Seigneur who came from Rosel Castle in Normandy and who had three reeds (roseaux) in his coat of arms. Every Seigneur of Rosel has had special duties to pay his Sovereign. Not only must he provide six carp to feed the royal guest but also he must obey the following injunctions to the last letter: 'If the king came to this isle, you shall ride into the sea to meet him till the waves reach the girth of your saddle; and likewise you shall see him off at his departure. And, as long as he tarry in the Isle, you shall act as his Butler, and receive as your fee what the king's Butler hath.'

The last time a Seigneur of Rosel had to play the part of the butler was in 1922, when King George V visited Gorey Castle. But when Queen Elizabeth II came to Jersey in 1978 the then Seigneur, Brigadier Raoul Lemprière-Robin and the Seigneur of Augrès, who enjoys similar rights, were the first people to greet Her Majesty at the harbour after she had been welcomed by the Lieutenant-Governor and Bailiff. They were also the last to bid her farewell before the Lieutenant-Governor and the Bailiff made their adieux. The idea behind this ancient privilege was to have the ear of your Sovereign to give your version of events both before and after possibly rival landowners had given theirs!

Equally dominating the parish is Gorey Castle or Mont Orgueil as it is also known. Fortress, Governor's residence, it was also a prison for defaulting Islanders and a most desperate one. In 1274 it is reported that one prisoner had lost the use of his legs and another the soles of his feet, because they had been kept so long in chains. Even the Bailiff himself, when made a prisoner there by the Governor in 1494, fared no better. It is recorded that, 'He died there covered with lice and vermin.' It was here that those to be tried for witchcraft were kept and sometimes died before their case could be heard.

There are also tales of heroism associated with the castle, such as during the Civil War when Lady de Carteret kept the Royal flag over it, while her husband was holding Elizabeth Castle, also for the King. There are horrifying tales, too, such as when two Parliamentarians, fearing they were to be hanged when the Royalists recovered Jersey, tried to escape. Chevalier gives the grim details of the fate of Dean Bandinel and his son in his Journal:

> With a gimlet, they bored holes through the plank of a door, and by boring them close together they brake that plank. The door led to another room, next to the outer wall, which had a closet, into which, by removing some stones, they crept with difficulty. Here was a narrow window, through which they had hard work to squeeze. Then, by the help of a cord and towels fastened to a kitchen ladle fixed in a crack in the wall, they began to climb down. The wall was high and terrifying to descend, and they chose a night when a fierce gale was blowing, and trees were torn up by their roots. At the foot of the wall was rugged rock sore difficult to clamber down. The son slid down first; but the rope was too short, and he fell on the rock and lay senseless. When the father was half way down, the rope snapped, and he crashed on the rock, and broke all his bones.

In the morning the Dean was discovered lying unconscious on the rocks – he died a few hours later. Though his son managed to crawl some distance from the castle he, too, was discovered and brought back, but before he could be hanged, he died of his injuries.

Trust a Jerseyman to take full advantage of a free offer! Until the mid-1800s, the place for Islanders to flock to on Easter Monday was Gorey Castle. Why? 'This being the only day of the year that free admission was given to the public. From midday to nightfall, all roads led to the castle and everybody went on foot.' There was also an Easter fair held at Gorey, which gave the ladies a splendid opportunity to show off their new outfits.

Gorey Castle had, in fact, been a centre to visit right from Catholic times. Inside the castle walls was the chapel dedicated to St George, therefore it became the custom to make a pilgrimage to Gorey on the Saint's Day, 23 April. So popular was this pilgrimage that the authorities deliberately kept down the number of those who could be within the castle walls at any one time – lest they suddenly took it into their heads to capture the castle!

This parish for many years now has been the only one to keep up the ancient custom of 'bannelais'. Throughout the year the road sweepings such as leaves and twigs are stacked at two places. The first is the main depot at the top of St Catherine's Hill and the second is at Carrefour Baudains.

Come October, the Constable turns himself into an auctioneer to get the best price he can from these 'bannelais' – or road sweepings. St Martin auctions the bannelais each year, whilst St Helier's bannelais is used by the Public Services Department.

The parish has had its fair share of 'charmers' over the years as the following stories will testify. Someone was once so afflicted with warts which nothing seemed to remove, that he went to the charmer. She did nothing to the warts but merely told the man 'Rub your hands on the ground on your way back.' He did just that and the warts disappeared.

On another occasion a young boy and his parents were taking tea with a St Martin family. Suddenly the young boy put his hand into the jug of hot water on the table. When the lady of the house saw what had happened, she called for someone to fetch 'Poppa' – a well-known charmer. When he came into the room, he gently took the boy's scalded and painful hand and began to soothe it. When he stopped, there was no sign at all that the boy's hand had been scalded, nor did he feel any more pain.

But if you want to find a 'charmer' or a white witch for yourself and your ailments, take heed from this story. A man who had visited a charmer in St Martin was full of praise for what she had done but when his companion asked where she lived, the first man shut up like a clam. When pressed further, all he would say was that she lived in a white cottage on a corner but he dare not give away more details for fear of being cursed.

Just as the Minquiers belong to Grouville Parish, so is the Ecréhous reef part of St Martin's Parish. In fact, the proximity to Jersey of both the mainland of France and reefs like the Ecréhous gave rise to the belief in La Chaussée des Boeufs, or the 'Legend of the Plank.' It told of a time when all that separated Jersey from France was a three-foot-deep stream between Les Boeufs Bank and La Rocque. This meant that whenever the Bishop of Coutances, in whose diocese Jersey once was, wanted to visit the Island, all he needed was a plank – to bridge the stream.

But, as De La Croix describes, this handy state of affairs came to an abrupt end:

In 709 there occurred a violent invasion [encroachment] by the sea of the forest which bounded the area of the Diocese of Coutances. A south-westerly wind, which blew incessantly for three months with great violence, overturned the trees in the direction of the wind and gathered together the waters from the Ocean in such quantities from our coasts that the March tides overstepped their ordinary limits and overwhelmed a large stretch of country. Nevertheless, it was only in 860, that all the forest was completely submerged and then the Islands of Jersey, Guernsey, and Alderney found themselves further away from the Continent than hitherto.

Later the Ecréhous became a great smuggling centre for profit-seeking Jerseymen. Or, when Jersey was politically and fanatically divided between the 'Charlots' and 'Magots', it was a convenient place on which to dump voters who supported the wrong party until election time was over!

Small as it is, twice in its history the Ecréhous has had a 'king'. The first was Philip Pinel, who, with his wife, was 'crowned' by Jersey fisherfolk who had huts on the reef in 1863. Twenty-one years later, the royal couple were described by P. Ouless as follows:

They have lived on the Ecréhous for 39 years, seldom visiting Jersey more than five or six times a year, when the king takes over the seaweed or 'vraic' that he has burnt and exchanges it for flour and other necessaries. This burnt vraic is valued highly by the Jersey farmers for manure, and by some of them is considered extremely good for promoting the growth of Jersey's principal industry, i.e. early potatoes). It must be burnt indoors, or otherwise it would soon be blown away and lose its goodness. A large sack of it sells for about four shillings. The King's palace consists of two huts, in one of which he cooks and lives, and in the other he keeps his stores, etc. These huts are built on the ridge of shingle on Blanc' Isle, but they are well protected by large rocks on each side. Still at very high spring tides the King and Queen have had to seek refuge with their 'bags and baggage' on Marmotier; as the old king says, 'The Sea put it there and the Sea can take it away again.' He is engaged in building with loose stones a kind of citadel of refuge on the rock north of his house. With more faith than, we thought, probability, he told us it would be ready next year, and he formally invited us to a house warming on that occasion. The only vegetation on Blanc' Isle is a few Marsh Mallow shrubs and some samphire, the latter of which, when soaked in salted water for a couple of hours and then placed in malt vinegar, makes a healthy and succulent pickle. The King told us that he had lived on the 'Main Land' when he first came to the Ecréhous. We were rather surprised when he pointed out the Maître Ile as the 'Main Land'; but then everything is relative!

The second self-styled king of the Ecréhous was Alphonse le Gastelois, whose tale is a pathetic one. It started when during the late 1950s and early 1960s there were several sexual attacks on young children. These usually took place at weekends, when the attacker would come into the children's bedrooms while the rest of the family slept and either assault them there or entice them out into a neighbouring field. In one horrific instance, the mother of a fourteen year-old girl was tied to a chair while her daughter was taken outside and sexually assaulted.

For ten years these attacks continued and the police seemed no nearer in tracking down the mystery attacker. But that did not stop Islanders drawing up their own list of suspects and in St Martin the name at the top was Alphonse le Gastelois. As an odd-job man, he was often to be seen

Alphonse le Gastelois of Ecréhous (The Islander)

128

cycling round the parish lanes in the afternoon and early evenings. It was said that he did not sleep at night, only during the day. In 1960 he was accused of approaching a woman, frightening her, following her and then running away. His sentence of a month's imprisonment, however, was quashed for lack of sufficient evidence. Later he was interviewed by the police for a total of over forty hours as the prime suspect for the sexual attacks on children.

Again, nothing could be proved against him. But the strain of being the centre of the neighbours' suspicious gossip was becoming too much to bear, so, urged on by a friend, he decided to leave Jersey. He also thought that if the next attack occurred in his absence, that would surely prove his innocence. For his self-imposed exile he chose the Ecréhous, with the second largest islet, Marmontier, as his base.

Alphonse le Gastelois's exile lasted fourteen years. During this time his only freshwater supply was rain; his food either what visitors brought to the reef, or what he found himself in the way of shellfish and seaweed. It was a Spartan existence but he survived. He had found refuge from malicious gossip, together with peace of mind and in his new-found freedom called himself 'King of the Ecréhous'. While he was there, the perpetrator of the sexual crimes against children was finally caught and convicted. His name was Edward John Louis Paisnel, better known to all Islanders as the 'Beast of Jersey' .

Cherchi la ville par le chalé
To go to town via Mont Orgueil Castle
(to do something in a roundabout way)

St Mary

This parish may have a smaller population than any of the other parishes but it can boast along its northern coast from Grève de Lecq to Mourier Valley some of the most breathtaking scenery in the island. Its coastline also includes many of Jersey's 300 caves, including that spectacular cliff formation known today as 'Devil's Hole'. This is a natural crater in the solid rock, about 100 feet across and 200 feet deep. It has been formed over the centuries by the sea continually washing away the soft rock and earth at the back of what was once a cave, until the hole appeared.

The origin of its name is harder to trace than its formation. Mr P. Ahier has found at least three possible sources, one arising from its original name 'Le Creux de Vis' – the Cave of the Bay. But 'Le Vier Vi' is a Jersiais nickname for the Devil and, as there was certainly a hole through the cave, 'trou du vi' or 'Trou du Diable' could eventually have been turned into the English 'Devil's Hole'.

More picturesque explanations were given to Mr Ahier by a schoolboy and Mr P.W. Arthur. The first told of how one of the Viking ships got wrecked near by and all that got washed ashore was the grotesque figure on its prow. This so resembled what the superstitious natives thought of as the Devil, that the place was ever after called 'Devil's Hole'. The second tale concerned the wrecking of a French ship in 1851. Its figurehead was washed straight into the hole. Then as Mr P. Arthur remembered, 'someone had a brain wave and called in Captain John Giffard, a well-known sculptor in his day from St Peter's Valley, to add the arms, legs etc. to the torso and thus the 'Devil' came into existence!

But the name might merely have come from the seemingly superhuman and eerie sounds of the water sucking in and surging out of the cave. Anyway, today's visitors can see a suitably horrific statue of the Evil One to the right of the narrow winding path that leads to his Hole.

To the west of the Devil's Hole is the small bay of Grève de Lecq, only half of which is in St Mary's Parish. Four miles out to sea from there is the reef which used to be called Les Pierres de Lecq. The reason for its change of name is a pitiful one.

In 1565, Elizabeth I gave the Seigneur of St Ouen, Helier de Carteret, the right to colonise Sark. So de Carteret chose thirty-five Jersey and five Guernsey families for the expedition. Tragically, on the journey across, one of the ships foundered on Les Pierres de Lecq and among those drowned were many young children. Their plaintive cries as the ship first struck the rocks can still be heard whenever there is to be a storm, and the sound is known as 'Le Cri de la Mer'. This sad tale so affected any sailors or fishermen sailing past the rocks, that they always used to say an 'Our Father' – a 'Pater Noster' – and the reef is now known, therefore, as the Paternoster Rocks.

Over the centuries the tranquillity of this parish, once famous for its peaceful sheep-breeding, has been broken by major differences of opinion between its Constables and Rectors. A particularly unpleasant quarrel erupted in 1626 between the Constable and Dean Bandinel, who was later to die in his escape attempt from Gorey Castle. The Dean had three accusations to

make: the first was of the Constable's 'presuming without any warrant or warning to command him not to preach that day, expelling the clerks, and causing the church to be shut up the whole day to the great scandal of the isle.'

But the Constable had done worse than that. He had thrust the Dean's wife out of the church at the point of a halberd and had gone on to profane the church and the Communion table 'with the blood of a dog, which he stabbed with a knife while the

Minister was preaching'.

Proof that the Church continued its strict watch over the morals of the Islanders – no matter how far away from St Helier they lived right into the eighteenth century, can be gathered from the following scene that took place in St Mary's Church in 1744. Elizabeth Robert presented herself, after the saying of the Nicene Creed, in front of the pulpit to the whole congregation. She was wearing a shroud, had bare legs and feet and carried a white wand in her hand. Then she went down on her knees and confessed her sin, and fully acknowledged the disgrace she had brought on her parish. After this public confession, if the Rector had thought that she was truly repentant, he would have publicly received her back into 'the peace of the Church'. And her sin? Elizabeth Robert had been reported drunk at a Christmas party!

St Ouen

 Perhaps the St Ouennais get their self-esteem from the fact that no less a man than William the Conqueror had as his most binding oath 'By St Ouen I swear it'. But who was this powerful Saint? He was really Dadon, who became Bishop of Rouen, the capital of William's Duchy of Normandy. His personal emblem was a cross of gold on a blue ground.

'Who says St Ouen says de Carteret', so the saying goes. And that is not surprising, considering that the de Carteret family has provided a continuous line of Seigneurs of St Ouen – the most senior of Jersey's Seigneurs – for the last 800 years. They survived French invasion; being on the Royalist side in the Civil War; and all attempts at English interference in Jersey affairs.

One of their prized possessions is the picture of a large black horse, whose spectacular leap saved a fifteenth-century de Carteret's life. During the French Occupation in the 1460s, Philippe de Carteret was suspected of leading a resistance movement and so the French were anxious to capture him. The story continues:

It befell one day that he went to fish in his pond near St Ouen's Bay, and the French came stealthily along the beach between the shingle and the sea, thinking to catch him unawares, and bring him captive to the Castle. But the Seigneur ever kept a good horse, and he sprang to the saddle, hoping to reach his manor. But, ere he could get to the crest of the hill, another troop appeared, striving to cut him off, and he was constrained to swerve towards the Val de la Charrière. Therefore, since he could not gain the end of the track, he made his horse leap the sunken road at its deepest place where it is twenty-two feet wide, and, spurring towards Les Landes, so made his escape. But ere he could reach the manor, his horse fell dead beneath him; whereat the Seigneur was sorely grieved, and he would not suffer it to be devoured by dogs or birds, but caused it to be buried in his garden for the good service it had done him.

A later de Carteret owed his life to the bravery of his wife. In 1494 another Philippe de Carteret had had the temerity to accuse the English Governor of Jersey of abusing his privileges. In revenge for his outspokenness, the Governor had a letter forged which suggested that de Carteret was, in fact, a traitor – he was planning to give over Gorey Castle to the French. When de Carteret protested his innocence, one of the Governor's henchmen challenged him to 'trial by battle'.

Until the day of the duel, the two men were kept in Gorey Castle, but, unknown to de Carteret – who was fed only on bread and water his opponent was being given the best of prison fare. Moreover the Governor forbad any Jersey boat to leave for England. He wanted to be the one to explain to Henry VII the exact circumstances in which Jersey's leading Seigneur now found himself, in order to circumvent royal displeasure.

When Margaret, the wife of de Carteret, heard what desperate straits her husband was in, she realised that the only hope was to get help from the King of England himself. So she got round the Governor's prohibition by asking a fisherman to take her as far as Guernsey and from there she took a cutter to Poole. Then she made the journey from Poole to the King's Court at Sheen by coach and horses – all this just a few days after having given birth to her twenty-first child. She arrived only twenty-four hours before the Governor did and so impressed was the King by her urgent bravery, that he agreed to let de Carteret be tried by the English Privy Council.

Margaret's next task was to get back to Jersey with the precious Royal Seal before the unequal 'trial by battle' took place. Good fortune was hers – she found a boat in Southampton that landed her in Jersey just the night before the battle. So she did indeed save her husband's life, for when he was eventually sent to Westminster for trial as a traitor, he was acquitted.

Such a happy ending was not the fate of twenty-year-old François Scornet. In March 1941 during the German Occupation of both France and the Channel Isles, he organised a party of French boys to sail from Brittany to join the Free French Forces in England. When they got as far as Guernsey they were delighted – they thought it was the Isle of Wight, and immediately began to sing the 'Marseillaise'. They were seized at once by the Germans and were sent to be tried in Jersey.

At his trial François Scornet took full responsibility for what had happened. So, for 'favouring the actions of the enemy by wilfully supporting England in the war against the German Empire', he was sentenced to death. His last letter to his parents read, 'My dear parents, my very dear parents, the end of my life is at hand. I am going to die for France, facing the enemy bravely. I forgive everyone. Vive la France. Vive Dieu. For the last time I embrace you.'

Then on 17 March he, a Catholic priest, and his coffin were taken by lorry to St Ouen's Manor. After receiving the Last Sacrament, he was stood in front of an oak tree in the Manor grounds and shot by a firing-squad. His death is commemorated each year on the spot where he so bravely died.

To the north of St Ouen's Manor used to stand the ruined Chapel of St Marie de Lec, which was once the scene of a secret wedding. In 1540, Edward de Carteret, aged twenty-two, was married to the widow of the richest man of the Island, old Michael Sarre, who had been buried only two weeks earlier. But their

The Old Tower, St Ouen's Manor (The Islander)

happiness was short-lived, because de Carteret was found to be the cause of Sarre's death. He had, apparently, burst into the bedroom, brutally assaulted the old man, thrown him into an empty room, which he secured with a rope, and had left him there to die of his injuries. He himself had spent the rest of the night with Sarre's wife. The case gained special notoriety because it was eventually heard before the infamous Star Chamber but the verdict was not recorded.

This parish also has the distinction of having lost one of its manors. The story of the submerged La Brecquette Manor off L'Etacq has had more than one chronicler. The earliest, a copy of which is to be found in the *Almanach de la Chronique de Jersey* states: 'In 1356, the sea engulfed a large area of fertile land in the Parish of St. Ouen. The accounts of the Exchequer mention the names of people who inhabited that locality. The forest of La Brecquette was overwhelmed and swallowed up by a terrible hurricane. In that year Jean Mathurins [Maltravers] was the warden [Governor] of the Island and William Hastein, the Bailiff.'

Then in 1669, at the hearing of a dispute between the Seigneurs of St Ouen's Bay, two witnesses gave details of the submerged manor and its forest. The first witness was Philip Mahaut, aged about eighty. He declared on oath that when he was a boy, he had been in the company of old people fishing at low tide, and had seen a quantity of stones belonging to Wallis: he had been informed by these people that they were the ruins of the former Castle of La Brecquette. He had also seen trees along the seashore which separated the two fiefs in question. The second witness Elie du

Heaume, aged about seventy, stated that he had heard that the Manor of La Brecquette lay to the north of a stream which went through a field called 'La Haussière'.

The whole story is summed up by the following seventeenth century account also quoted, as the above extracts are, in P. Ahier's *Stories of Jersey Seas*:

> The fiefs of Morville and Robillard were part of the fief St Germain in Jersey formerly belonging to John Wallis, Gent. His manor house was situated in this same fief, in the valley of l'Etacq, close to the seashore known as the Manor of La Brecquette, near which is a forest of oak trees both on the east and north sides of that manor which is now below the level of the high tide. The above valley and manor have, for several years, been lowered by the sea: nevertheless, at low tides the remains of this manor can be seen, and, after stormy weather, a quantity of oak tree stumps, which at one time flourished in the valley, are visible.

St Ouen is the parish where they like to be different. They used to be called 'Grey bellies', because they wore jerseys of natural wool, unlike the rest of the Islanders who wore navy ones. They also try to be the last to vote at an election. On their north-west coast line is the shrine at the 200 foot Pinnacle Rock, which was venerated for longer than any other holy place in Jersey – from about 2000 BC to AD 200. So it is not surprising that the biggest whale ever seen had to be washed up on their coastline. Dr Frank Le Maistre translates the story from Philippe Pirouet's eighteenth-century account:

> In the Year One Thousand Seven Hundred Twenty Six the 24th Day of December was found in Jersey at St Ouen at the haven of Le Pulec a big Fish which one calls Whale which had 71 feet in length and they made much oil from it for Burning the Seigneur of Vinchelais de Bas put Himself in Possession saying that she [the whale] was On his fief and for Souvenir caused to be taken the two Bones of the Jaws which he caused to be attached at the two Sides of the Big Gate of the yard of His

Manor & Are visible to be seen to those who will not be able to believe it there were several persons who took away Bones from the backbone of the said Fish to their House which Serve to sit them.

Tangible evidence of this extraordinary tale exists to this day. Parts of the jawbones of the huge whale still stand at either side of the main road gateway of Le Manoir de Vinchelez de Bas.

Cabbage-stalk walking sticks on sale in St. Helier in the early years of this century

Nor is it surprising to find White Ladies haunting lanes in St Ouen such as La Rue à la Pendue (Hanged Man's Lane). George d'La Forge, in the translation of his letter to the *Jersey Evening Post* on 2 December 1982, tells of a sighting at the turn of the century. When he was nine years old, in 1900, a neighbour rushed into his grandparents' home one night and asked for the Centenier to be fetched. 'I've just seen La Blianche Femme. She was in La Rue à la Pendue. She jumped from the hedge behind me, not far from the lay-by. I took to my heels but the faster I went the faster she ran after me. I don't know what I would have done if I hadn't seen you were still up, as I'm out of breath and almost ready to faint.'

George's grandfather escorted the distraught woman home and then explained to his grandson: 'There are still people around who believe in witchcraft, ghosts and superstitions of every imaginable sort.... Fortunately people are beginning to be more enlightened on the subjects of ghosts and phantoms. But La Rue à la Pendue and the road running between the manors at Vinchelez are still the haunts of the so-called Blianches Femmes, as they have the reputation of having been haunted from the very earliest days.' Other people can remember Vinchelez Lane as being the haunt of copper-faced soldiers.

Recently on Radio Jersey there was told the charming story of a unicorn seen wandering in St Ouen. It even had its likeness made in wood at L'Etacq – but that legend is still growing!

In the realm of non-fiction, L'Etacq is one of the few places on the Island where the traditional Jersey Cabbage walking stick can still be found. Once upon a time a whole shop would be devoted to the sale of this formerly popular fashion accessory.

St Peter

This parish, with the keys of heaven its emblem, has war relics within its boundaries that span 400 years. The first is the Houndsditch-made cannon at Beaumont Crossroads which dates from Tudor times and of which there are only two of its kind still in existence. It bears the inscription JHON OWEN MADE THIS PESE ANNO DNI 1551 FOR THE PARYSHE OF SAYNT PETER IN JERSSE.

But it was also here that Oliver Cromwell's nine-year domination of Jersey began. The Roundhead Admiral Blake, with a fleet of eighty ships, sailed between L'Etacq and St Brelade for two whole days. All the while the Jersey Royalist forces were marching back and forth ready to repel them should they attempt to land. This they eventually did, just before midnight to the south of St Ouen's Pond. After a fierce battle, Carteret retreated his Jersey forces to Elizabeth Castle. Blake and the Roundheads were the Island's conquerors from 1651 to 1660.

The parish church has the unique distinction of having a red light on the top of its spire to warn aircraft of its presence as they fly to or from Jersey's airport, but its parishioners witnessed an even stranger sight in 1552. At a time when all objects of Popery were strictly forbidden, Mary Falle was seen going into church carrying her rosary. The Constable went up to her and told her to hand the rosary to him immediately. She refused. When the case was heard, the sentence given was that Mary Falle's husband, Pierre, should be sent to prison for allowing his wife to behave in such an idolatrous way!

At the end of the seventeenth century the church was at the centre of a bitter quarrel between its Rector and the Parish Constable. The Rector, Dean Le Couteur, wanted to celebrate Holy Communion on Christmas Day as well as on the four Sundays laid down by ecclesiastical law. The Constable and the Churchwardens would not hear of any such extra Communion – not on doctrinal grounds, but because the parish would have to pay for the extra wine needed!

The Dean was so furious at this unreasonable prohibition, that he excommunicated them all, but his accusations against the Constable and Churchwardens were so slanderous that they, in their turn, charged him with defamation of character. The unholy contretemps resulted in the old Dean being sent to prison.

That the parish had its more caring side is evinced by its Leper House and its Grammar School. In medieval times when lepers were the feared outcasts of society, there was a special home for Jersey lepers sited near the house called 'Oak Walk'. It had its own chapel, dedicated to St Nicholas, and King John himself had given it a grant from the royal revenue of Ruaval Mill in Grouville.

The Grammar School was built at the end of the fifteenth century by two Jerseymen who had made good on the mainland. They had it built next to the ancient Chapel of St Anastase from which it took its name and it was to serve bright boys from the western parishes. The school had a chequered career but survived until the middle of the last century.

Anyone visiting St Peter might wonder why it has a 'Cinders' Crossroads but, in fact, Carrefour à Cendres is a corruption of Carrefour Alexandre – the name of a family in the parish. It also has a strange legend attached to it. A woman was going home one day past the Carrefour when she heard a piteous meowing. Searching round, she saw a tiny kitten under the hedge, so out of pity she picked it up to take it home with her. However as she walked along the tiny kitten began to grow in size; it weighed more and more heavily in her arms. Thoroughly frightened, the woman tried to put the heavy burden down – it would not leave her arms. So in utter desperation she retraced her steps to the Carrefour so that she could put the animal back where she had found it. To her amazement the kitten began to grow smaller again, until, when she placed it carefully back under the hedge – it vanished altogether.

Cat qui s'laue au d'sus l'ouotheille, ch'est seigne depluie.
When a cat licks itself aboue the ear, it is a sign of rain.

St Saviour

Lillie Langtry is not the only lady commemorated in the parish of her birth. The fairies, too, were remembered by the superstitious who gave the name La Rue à la Dame to the hill that runs down from Five Oaks to Grand Vaux. Une Dame, or fairy, apparently once lived in the prehistoric remains at the foot of the hill, which, even today, is still supposed to be haunted.

Two riding accidents are also recalled in the parish. The first is by the name of 'La Fosse à L'Ecrivain' – the lawyer's grave. Legend has it that the lawyer had been visiting friends in the country and on his way back to St Helier was thrown by his horse. He fell into a deep ditch by the side of the road and died there. That same night there was a violent rain-storm which caused the sides of the ditch to fall in and cover the body, so that it was not found till some time later. Less dramatically, some authorities believe that the area took its name from a local family, named either Scriven or Scrivain who lived thereabouts in the sixteenth century.

The second riding tragedy is marked by a cross erected in Grand Vaux on the spot where the accident took place. It was erected in 1928 by the then Seigneur of Trinity, the famous Churchman Athelstan Riley, in memory of his daughter-in-law who was killed when she fell from her horse.

Although St Saviour has the shortest coastline of all the parishes, it has within its boundaries the famous Rocher des Proscrits – the Exiles' Rock. The commemorative stone erected on it by La Société Jersiaise tells of it being the spot where Victor Hugo and fellow European exiles mulled over Revolutionary and other weighty matters.

The parish church was originally four small, unconnected chapels, only one of which was dedicated to St Saviour of the Thorn. This dedication suggests that the relic held there was supposed to be either a thorn from Christ's Crown of Thorns, or one from the sacred thorn bush at Glastonbury. This was said to have taken root when Joseph of Arimathaea planted the stick, which he had cut in the Garden of the Resurrection, in English soil. The Crown of Thorns is in the parish emblem anyway, together with the three nails which secured Christ's hands and feet to the Cross.

In the sixteenth century the 'wicked Seigneur of Longueville Manor' lived in this parish. His name was Hostes Nicolle and he was also the Island's Bailiff. Not content with these positions and all the fiefs he possessed, he coveted the land and property of a poor butcher who lived next door to him and tried to think up a way of getting it for himself. Then, as the chronicler relates, one day he found a way:

> He bade his servants slay two of his finest sheep, and carried them to the poor man's house, who was a butcher by trade. Next day he roused the Constable and his officers, and bade them search the butcher's house, where they found the sheep dead and hanging in a stable, where the Bailiff's servants had put them. The man was at once arrested, and brought into Court, and without defence condemned to be hanged that day, though he was in no wise guilty. As the hangman put the rope round his neck at the door of the Court, he said to the Bailiff before everyone, 'I summon you to appear within forty days before the just Judge of all to answer for this injustice.' And on the thirty-ninth day that unjust judge fell dead by the wayside, as he was returning from Town.

The name of the butcher was Anthoine and one of the fields near Longueville Manor still has the name Le Pré d'Anthoine and was owned for many centuries by members of his family.

There are other stories about the Manor that the novelist Eleanor Glyn loved to hear her Jersey landlady tell her. There was the La Cloche family of Longueville who had died out because of this wronged neighbour's terrible curse. Then, when Mr Venables (who was Seigneur of the Manor while she was in the island) lay dying, it is reported that the clattering hooves of phantom horses were distinctly heard in the courtyard.

A spooky tale is also told about the road that connects the Bagatelle and Bagot Road – Les Varines. It was the favourite walk of a young couple but the man always resisted stopping at one particular spot along it – he felt there was something strange about it. Only later did he find out that someone in the neighbourhood had brought some Egyptian mummies home with him from his travels abroad. His wife objected so strongly to having them in the house that he had buried them in one of his fields. This field was adjacent to the very spot in Les Varines which had felt so uncanny.

Recently a young girl and her family moved to a different house in the parish. On one of the first nights she spent in her new bedroom, she distinctly saw the outline of an old man floating above her bed. She did not feel at all frightened and when she told the rest of the family, they felt that it could only have been a good ghost, because their cat had stayed in the bedroom the whole time it appeared; but it has never been seen again.

Trinity

Trinity Church was originally dedicated to La Sainte Trinité and so the large initials PFSD on the parish badge stand for Pater, Filius, Spiritus Sanctus and Deus.

The church is not only sited on high ground but has a magnificent spire. This has the dubious record of having been the target for lightning no less than three times in nineteen years. In 1629 a large part of it was destroyed – a sure sign of 'God's wrath' at 'the pontifical grandeur of the Dean', thought the diarist Chevalier! Over twelve feet of the spire went when it was struck again in 1646. This damage had only just been repaired, when a thunderbolt – which also holed the roof and shattered all the glass windows – crashed it all down as far as the belfry. Only 300 years later did anyone think of installing a lightning-conductor!

When in 1558 René le Hardy, who was wanted for stealing, fled to the church for sanctuary, the Bailiff ignored the tradition which allowed him to do so and had him arrested. At the next meeting of the Royal Court the Dean and the Rectors made such a to-do about the Bailiff's breach of this ancient privilege of the Church, that the Royal Court gave way. It spared Le Hardy his life and allowed him to leave the Island.

In the same century, in its churchyard, there was an unusual funeral by torchlight. Sir Edouard de Carteret, a Trinity parishioner, had died on a visit to St Ouen's Manor, so plans were made to bury him in St Ouen's Church. However, just as the funeral procession was about to start, there was a sudden clap of thunder. The six horses who were pulling the hearse were so frightened that they bolted – pulling the hearse behind them – and did not stop until they reached Trinity Church. The mourners who had followed this incredible cross country funeral procession, then decided that what had happened was a sign that Sir Edouard wanted to be buried in his own parish, so a grave was hastily dug and the funeral service eventually finished by torchlight.

Another death-wish explains the legend of the heart which is said to lie in a casket under the cross in the grounds of Trinity Manor. When a seventeenth-century Seigneur, Amice de Carteret, died in St Loo, he asked for his heart to be embalmed and sent back to Jersey and buried in the grounds of his Manor. To underline the veracity of the legend, when the De Carteret grave in Trinity Church was opened, a casket containing an embalmed heart was found there.

With this legend obviously in mind, Athelstan Riley, father of the then Seigneur, made a similar request. He asked for his body to be buried in Trinity, but for his heart to be cut out and sent to Cornwall with which he had close associations. As his son said, 'I made my father promise me that I wouldn't be expected to carry out any such bizarre request on his behalf!'

The most famous and romantic Trinity Manor story centres round Charles II when, as Prince of Wales – on the run from the Roundheads – he spent ten weeks in Jersey. The tale goes that the young Prince behaved cavalierly towards Marguerite, sister of Amice de Carteret, the then Seigneur of Trinity. From this dalliance was supposed to have sprung a certain Jacques La Cloche. Even further claims are made that La Cloche and Dumas's fictitious *Man in the Iron Mask* were indeed one and the same man. To add to the mystery, believers in the story point out that a page is missing from the Trinity Parish register. Did the missing page record the illegitimate royal birth?

Unfortunately for all the novelists who have made Marguerite one of Charles II's many mistresses, there is not a shred of evidence to prove the affair. The page torn from the register is for 1648 – two years after the Prince's short stay in Jersey. He did, though, stay at Trinity Manor, and a copy of the Lely royal portrait, given in gratitude for the Seigneurial hospitality afforded him, now hangs in what is known as the 'Chambre du Roi'. From this bedroom window  can be seen a later replacement of the great turkey oak beneath which Charles was meant to have sat, as well as the large stone table under it, at which he was supposed to have feasted.

One of the duties that still has to be carried out by the Seigneur of Trinity is to offer a pair of mallard ducks to the visiting Monarch. For this purpose ducks are always reared in readiness on the manorial ponds. However on the Queen's visit in the summer of 1976, things did not go according to plan, as the Seigneur admitted. 'My own ducks' plumage wasn't very colourful at that time of year, so I had to beg two off Gerald Durrell!'

Two strange stories are associated with the Trinity area, the first far less well known than the second. A man was walking down a lane in the parish when out from behind a tree stepped a woman all dressed in white. She accompanied him along the road but said not a word to him and always kept her eyes on the road ahead. He tried to touch her to get her attention but some supernatural force seemed to be holding back his arm. After a while he decided to return home – along the same route that he had come. La Blanche Dame turned round, too, and when they got as far as the large tree, she stepped off the road and disappeared behind it.

Everyone in Jersey, though, has heard of Le Chien de Bouley –

the dog of Bouley – but no one is quite sure of how the legend of this monstrous black dog with huge saucer eyes sprang up. As it was supposed to roam the lanes round Bouley Bay, was it a figment of the smugglers' imagination to keep fearful Islanders out of the way while they carried on their important business?

Or is the Jersey Norman French 'Le Tchan du Bouôle' a corruption of 'Le Chouan du Bouôle' – the French Royalist of Bouley Bay? For when the Revolutionaries seized power in France at the end of the eighteenth century, many émigrés sought refuge in Jersey. And they were particularly fond of playing practical jokes on the natives so it is possible that one of them dressed up as a dog for the sheer fun of seeing the Islanders run for their lives! Whatever the origin, anyone who sees an enormous dog with equally enormous eyes, padding up and down the cliff paths at night, can be certain of one thing – there is going to be a storm! A much more recent sighting on Bouley Bay Hill has been the cyclists. They ride their pedal bikes through the hedge, across the road and through the opposite hedge as if the hedges were not there.

Even more sinister on that rugged north coast of Bouley Bay is the cave that used to be called the 'good' – Le Creux Bouanne – but which after 1462 was only referred to as 'The Place Accursed'. It was the time of the Norman occupation of the eastern half of Jersey by sheep stealing brigands known as 'Moutonniers'.

In a Jersey farm on the western slopes of Bouley Bay there was a double celebration. Not only was it 'L'Assise de Veille' – the first of the knitting and social evenings of the winter – but also a betrothal feast. The rich farmer's son, Raulin de L'Ecluse, was to marry a neighbour, Jeanne de Jourdain. There were many toasts to the future happiness of the young pair and then they raised their cider cups in the fervent wish of everyone present: 'A bas touos les pendars de Normands' – 'Down with all the gallows fodder of Normans.'

At that moment there was a loud hammering on the door. Everyone wondered who it could be at that time of night – no one wanted to go to the door in case it was one of the occupation force – a Moutonnier. The knock came again – more imperiously. The old farmer went to open the door and then were heard the hateful tones of a Norman voice. In came a broad-shouldered brutal-looking man. He wanted to know why he had been kept waiting so long outside the door, what they were all doing together. Were they conspiring to overthrow their conquerors? Just in case they were, he said, he would like to see them all down on their knees in front of him. Nobody moved. He turned to the old farmer, 'Tell them to kneel,' he roared.

Young Raulin could no longer control his anger. Pointing to the door, 'Get out, before I throw you out,' he hissed. The Norman's hand reached swiftly for the dagger at his side – but then it stopped. A devilish smile began to cross his coarse features: 'You shall pay dearly for this, young cockerel. Alright, I shall go now, but rest assured I'll be back, and, what is more, tomorrow you will be swinging in chains from the walls of Gorey Castle.'

The festivities continued, despite the threat, and soon after midnight Raulin saw Jeanne home. As they took tender leave of each other, Raulin noticed how pensive and low his fiancée looked and asked why she seemed so sad. 'I don't know,' she replied. 'I just have this feeling of foreboding that something fearful is going to happen.' Then she took hold of his arm. 'Look, Raulin, see how threatening the sky looks. Don't you think if there is going to be a storm that it would be wiser for you to stay here overnight with me and my grandparents?' Even as she spoke, a flash of lightning outlined the sombre shape of the cliffs lashed by the sea that boiled below them.

But Raulin saw no reason for a mere storm to prevent him returning home, despite Jeanne's fears, and turned to go. 'At least take Fidèle with you. He's such a plucky dog, that if there were any danger he'd be there to help you,' his fiancée pleaded. Still laughing at her gloomy thoughts, yet wanting to please her, he agreed to take Fidèle.

So, with the thunder overhead reverberating and thrown back at them by the cliffs of the Tombelènes, Raulin and the dog walked as swiftly as they could back to the farm. Suddenly Fidèle stopped and started to whimper, and then Raulin, above the noise of the storm, began to hear what the dog had heard – the steady beat of horses' hooves coming in their direction down the lane.

A yellow flash of light showed the horsemen to be none other than some Norman Moutonniers. 'Out stealing more sheep?' asked Raulin rashly. Immediately one of the Normans slashed his whip across Raulin's face, another two caught hold of him and pushed him roughly to the ground. When Fidèle went for Raulin's attackers, he was savagely thrust at with a dagger. But before Raulin was tied up and thrown over a saddle as their prisoner, he was able to urge the wounded dog to go to fetch help.

Bundled up and blindfolded, Raulin was jogged along until he heard the sound of shingle under the horses' hooves. Then he was seized and thrown into what he guessed was – by its feel of dampness and strange echo – a cave. After his captors had noisily and greedily eaten and drunk their fill, they dragged him forward, unbound and unblindfolded him and pushed him towards their Chief.

The two men recognised each other immediately. Raulin was face to face with none other than the Norman brigand he had ordered from his father's house only three hours before. His captor could not conceal his delight at who he had before him, completely in his power. 'What shall we do with the prisoner?' he shouted at his men. 'Kill him,' they drunkenly shouted back. 'Certainly a brave act,' Raulin commented sarcastically 'two dozen to one. But you shall see that a Jerriais knows how to die.' So precipitous then was the Normans' surge forward with daggers upraised to kill him, that the table they sat at was pushed over. But their Chief held up his hand to stop them. 'To kill him this way is too good a death for him. Let him die like a dog – hung from the roof of the cave.'

While hasty preparations were being made in the Creux Bouanne for Raulin's death, his fiancée was already being led by the faithful dog to Carrefour des Crones, where Raulin had urged the dog back for help. Fidèle had gone straight back to Jeanne and by his continually whimpering and going to the door had persuaded the girl to get up. When Jeanne patted the dog to quieten him he had given a howl of pain. Then she saw – blood on her hand, on the floor and a gaping wound in the dog's neck. Without further ado she unlocked the door and followed the dog into the storm to see what horror had befallen Raulin. Soon the dog had picked up the scent from Carrefour des Crones and unerringly led his mistress across the beach, and to the deep gash in the rugged cliffs of the Tombelènes – Creux Bouanne. There, to her terror. She saw Raulin with his hands tied behind him, a hangman's noose dangling over his head and – towering in front of him – the Norman who had prophesied his death. Jeanne without further hesitation, dashed into the cave, threw her arms round her lover's neck and facing the Normans cried out 'kill me too'. Raulin at first could not believe that this was not some dream. When he realised that it was indeed Jeanne, his agony only increased. 'Jeanne,' he groaned, 'don't you see that you are risking your precious life without being able to save mine?' 'There would be no life for me without you, we will die together,' was her only reply.

However the Chief of the Moutonniers, seeing Jeanne's beauty, had other ideas. 'Get on with the hanging, but do not touch the turtle dove – she is mine.' As two men came forward to do their Chief's bidding, Jeanne suddenly took the dagger from one of them, while Fidèle leapt at the throat of the other. Fidèle hung on to his mistress's assailant until he had no more strength left in him, then fell to the floor of the cave – dead. In the confusion Jeanne then cut Raulin's bonds and he immediately placed himself, unarmed as he was, in front of her. At this the Chief of the brigands decided to put an end to the unequal struggle and, with a brutal cry, slashed his dagger into Raulin's heart. Without a sound the young man fell dead at Jeanne's feet. Her immediate shriek of horror was so intense, so piercing, that it echoed and re-echoed her grief from side to side of the cave. Then she thrust her dagger deep into the Norman Chief's throat and, like one insane, rushed along the beach till she stood opposite L'Islet.

The Normans who had dashed after her, then saw her in a flash of lightning. She was standing on the top of L'Islet with her long black hair and cloak streaming in the wind, with her arms outstretched as if in supplication towards the sea. Then surging towards her, up sprayed a monstrous wave. As it went over her, again that terrible piercing cry – the Cry of the Tombelènes. Jeanne's body was later found floating in the sea: some carrion crows led two fishermen to Creux Bouanne, to those others who had taken their part in the awesome tragedy. That same day the two lovers were buried in holy ground but the brigand Chief was left for the crows to finish off. A year later, a priest was called to give the last rites to a Norman who had received a mortal wound in a quarrel. On his death-bed, the man confessed that he had once belonged to the notorious Moutonniers and gave the priest all the cruel details of what had happened that night in the Creux Bouanne. That is why it now has the name of 'The Place Accursed'.

Some Sovereign Remedies

*I*f Jersey in time past had fearful places and people to be beware of, there were always charms and spells to keep off the Evil Eye. A small spot of quicksilver in a locket worn round the neck, or an acorn in the pocket were ideal preventions against witchcraft. Should you have had the misfortune to be bewitched already, there was no need to despair. All you needed was a perfectly clean plate and the heart of an animal. Then you stabbed thorns, new nails or pins into the heart, declaiming a counter-charm as you did so.

Should affairs of the heart have been your problem, then 21 December, St Thomas's Day, could have been your lucky day – if you were a girl. Just before you got into bed, you had to walk backwards towards it holding a golden pippin in your hand. Then you put the apple under your pillow and as you got into bed you said aloud,

> *The Day of St Thomas,*
> *The shortest and the lowest,*
> *God, in sleeping, let me see*
> *The man who will love me.*
> *Show me my husband,*
> *The house where I shall live,*
> *The nation, and the country*
> *Where his home will be*
> *Such as he is, I shall love him.*
> *So be it.*

Into your dreams would then appear the man you would eventually marry, and if you had obeyed the ritual to the letter, before you had known where you were, he would not have been able to help himself from proposing to you.

Once you were engaged it was just as well not to be too thorough with the housework, but to be specially welcoming to all spiders. For every cobweb you saw as you woke in the morning meant a kiss from your fiance.

Perhaps today is one of those days when everything goes wrong. You were just about to avoid stepping under a ladder, when a St Helier traffic jam forced you to. Just by spitting through the rungs of the ladder you can completely escape the bad luck coming to you. If you have been in such a tizz-wozz that you have put your socks or tights on inside-out that, at least, is something you have done right. Inside-out hose are lucky – providing you do not put them back on again the right way, after you have discovered your mistake.

If you want good fortune for the rest of the month, then look at the moon from outside the house and over the right shoulder. If you strike any pockets you may have on you at the time – they could fill with money before the month is out.

Should your future plans include a holiday abroad and you want to avoid being delayed by Jersey fog, arriving to find your hotel only half-built and being fed inedible foreign food, then get a friend to throw an old shoe after you as you set off. That really should ensure you 'Bon Voyage'.

But perhaps you are proper poorly with a bad chest or whooping cough. Have you thought of trying snail syrup? All you need are twelve live snails, half a pound of moist brown sugar and one muslin bag. Your first job, once you have collected your snails, is to shell them, taking great care not to wound them too much, as they have to be alive to work themselves into the sugar. You then put them and the sugar into the muslin bag. This you hang over a basin to catch the resulting syrup. It is so effective that four teaspoonsful a day should be quite enough!

Should your problem be a nasty inflammation or a burn, then your neighbourly farmer is the man to seek. Ask him for as much cow dung as you would need to cover the offending place and keep the dung on overnight. When you remove the dung, the swelling will have gone.

Perhaps, though, you and the whites of your eyes have turned yellow. So prepare yourself for a journey to St Ouen. Find the house that is right next to the front gates of the parish church and look for the thorn bush growing just inside the front wall. Then politely ask the owner if you may take a small piece from it. Once home, scrape the thorn wood into a bowl, cover with white cognac and allow to stand overnight. Strain the ensuing concoction through muslin and drink a full wine glass of it twice a day.

Now, nobody likes warts and everybody wants to get rid of them. Nothing simpler – in fact you have a choice. Either you get a stalk of milkweed and squeeze it over the wart, or you do something a little more risky. When your local butcher is not looking, you steal a piece of raw meat, rub it on the wart and take particular care to throw the stolen meat away over your shoulder. Whichever method you choose, your warts should disappear.

There is something, however, that no Jersey person who wants to remain healthy should ever be without – D's Ortchies. Stinging nettle tea is quite simple to make. Once you have gathered the nettle tops, cut them up finely and put them in a non-aluminium saucepan with sufficient cold water to cover them. You merely bring them to the boil and simmer for half an hour.

With your stinging-nettle tea ready at your side, you either rub it in or drink it, according to what is wrong with you. If you have pleurisy, apply it to your side as hot as you can bear it. If your problem is fistulas, gangrene, manginess or itch in any part of the body, then rub it in. Should you feel lethargic, a little tea mixed with a little salt rubbed gently into the forehead should soon wake you up.

A drink of nettle tea has many benefits. It is good for anyone of any age who wishes 'to change the blood and carry away the phlegmatic superfluities in the body that winter has left behind.' As well as ameliorating blood-pressure, rheumatism and shingles, it also 'opens pipes and passages of lungs and so cures wheezing and shortness of breath and loosens tough phlegm'. It also works wonders with gouty pains. As a gargle it will get down any swellings in your throat in no time at all.

Apportez de siez vous, siez nous;
Mais n'emportez pon de siez nous, siez vous.

Bring from your place to our place;
But do not take from our place to your place.

If green fingers are your desire but your Jersey Royals have not come up to standard, have you made the grave error of getting your seed potatoes from the east? If so, your remedy is to remember the wise saw: 'Seed potatoes taken east do best.'

Then, as so much in life depends on the weather, keep your eyes on the Jersey cow. Whether she is wearing her coat or not, if she starts licking the hoof of a back foot it is going to rain. If you see a whole field of cows lying down on their right sides, then hurry home and fetch in the washing. Another way to be one up on the neighbours when it comes to planning alfresco outings is to take careful note of what kind of weather the first twelve days of January bring. If, for example, 6 January starts wet and then clears up in the afternoon, the first half of the sixth month, June, will also be wet, while the weather will be much brighter in the second half of the month. In some parishes they prefer to go by the weather during the twelve days of Christmas for their prophecies.

The most sovereign remedy of all, though, is the Royal Touch. It is specially effective if your problem is 'Les Ecrouelles' or scrofula. The last Sovereign to cure Jersey people of this dread malady was Charles II. Once in 1649 and twice in 1650 he cured several people who knelt before him by touching them on the throat and saying, 'God cure thee'. When will our Sovereign Queen Elizabeth II next be visiting Jersey?

There is just one extra tip to make your home secure against any Evil Eye. Take your front-door key, heat it until it is red-hot and no harm will ever come to anyone in your home. So, with all these sovereign remedies at your disposal, you should now be able to enjoy Jersey at its sunny best.

BIBLIOGRAPHY

Ahier, J. *Tableaux Historiques de la Civilisation à Jersey*, Le Livre, 1852.

Ahier, P. 'Old Jersey Customs', *Jersey Life* (May, June, Dec),1966.

Ahier, P. & Ashworth, W. *A Short Parochial & Commercial History of Jersey*, Ashton & Denton, 1977.

Ahier P. *Stories of Jersey Seas*, Advertiser Press Huddersfield, 1955, 1956, 1957.

Anon *Les Chroniques de Jersey 1585* (Ed.: Mourant), 1895.

Balleine, G.R. *Bailiwick of Jersey* (Revised J. Stevens), La Société Jersiaise, 1970.

Balleine, G.R. *History of the Island of Jersey*, Staples Press, 1950.

Balleine, G.R. 'Witch Trials in Jersey', *La Société Jersiaise Bulletin*, 1939.

Bertino, S. *Guide de la Mer Mysterieuse*, Editions Maritime et d'Outre Mer, 1970.

Bisson, S. *Jersey Our Island*, Batchworth Press, 1950.

Carey, E. *The Channel Islands*, A & C Black, 1904.

Chevalier, J. 'Le Journal' 1643-51, La Société Jersiaise, 1915.

Coysh, V. *The Channel Isles*, David & Charles, 1977.

Dalido *Ile Agricole Anglo Normande*, A. Chaumeron, 1951.

Dewar S. *Witchcraft and the Evil Eye in Guernsey*, Toucan Press, 1968.

Falle, P. *Caesarea. An Account of Jersey*, 1734.

Gastineau, E. *Hobble Through the Channel Islands in 1858*, Westerton, 1860.

Gruyer, P. *Victor Hugo Photographs*, Mendel,1905.

Hammond, R. *Guide to the Channel Isles*, Ward Lock, 1970.

Hugo, V. *Toilers of the Sea* (trans. W. May), Dent, 1961.

Islander Magazine, Guernsey Press, Various Issues. Jersey Catholic Record, 1971-74.

Jersey Evening Post, JEP, Various Issues.

Jersey Evening Post Almanac & Trade Directory, JEP, Various Issues.

Jersey Island Federation of Women's Institutes, *Bouan Appetit*, JEP, La Forge G. d' Letters to the Jersey Evening Post, JEP, Various.

L'Amy, J. *Jersey Folk Lore*, Bigwood, 1927.

Lemprière R. *Customs, Ceremonies & Traditions of the Channel Islands*, Robert Hale, 1976.

MacCulloch, E. *Guernsey Folk Lore*, F. Clarke Guernsey, 1903.

Maugham, R. *The Island of Jersey Today*, Madison & Co. Mead R. Jersey, Modern Guides Jersey Ltd.,1976.

Mollet, R. A *Chronology of Jersey*, La Societe Jersiaise, 1954.

Mourant, B. Jersey Costume Thesis, unpublished,1970.

Nicolle, E. The Town of St. Helier, Bigwood,1972.

Ouless, P. *The Ecréhous*, Jersey Chronique,1884.

Pitts, J. *Witchcraft & Devil Lore in the Channel Islands*, Guilles-Alles Libraire, 1886.

Plees, W. An Account of the Island of Jersey, T. Baker, 1817.

Poingdestre, J. Caesarea or A Discourse on the Island of Jersey 1682, La Société Jersiaise, 1889.

Ragg, A. Popular History of Jersey, W. E. Guiton, 1895.

Rutherford, W. Jersey, David & Charles, 1976.

Saunders, A.C. Chevalier and His Times, Bigwood, 1937.

Saunders, A.C. Jersey Before & After the Norman Conquest of England, Bigwood, 1935.

Saunders, A.C. *Jersey in the 15th & 16th Centuries*, Bigwood, 1933.

Sinel, J. *Prehistoric Times: Channel Islands*, Bigwood, 1923.

La Société Jersiaise Bulletins, La Société Jersiaise, Various.

Stead, J. *A Picture of Jersey*, 1809.

Stevens, C., Arthur J., Stevens J. *Jersey Place Names*, unpublished, 1975.

Stevens, J. *History of Longueville Manor*, Bigwood, 1982.

Stevens, J. *Old Jersey Houses I*, La Société Jersiaise, 1972.

The author and publishers are grateful to the following who kindly allowed the use of their illustrations: *Jersey Evening Post*; La Société Jersiaise; *The Islander*; St Helier Public Library; J. Stevens; BBC Radio Times Picture Library; Mary Evans Picture Library; Barreau Art Gallery, Jersey Museum; Carole Owens. Photographs on pages 77 and 110 courtesy Arthur Lamy. Cover photograph courtesy Stuart Abraham.

INDEX

(References in bold refer to illustrations)